Translation and Transgression in the Art of Shirin Neshat

I0473421

Precisely 30 years after the debut of her provocative photo-portraits, this book chronicles the early career of Iranian-American artist Shirin Neshat. In its first 20 years, Neshat's work weaved viewers into complex readings of women and power in Iran. Yet her images also drew criticisms of exoticizing Muslim women, and later video installations were accused of lacking political assertion during stormy relations between the West and the Islamic world.

Now broadly recognized as a social justice artist, this volume chronicles Neshat's evolution from photography to film, from personal to political expression, and expands existing scholarship to investigate underserved contexts for her work, including the cinematic turn and emergent theories of globality in contemporary art. Neshat's hyphenated identity was often attenuated by reductive and exoticizing discourses; therefore, this volume draws attention to her transnational methodologies, informed by strategies of appropriation, performativity, and embodiment while articulating Persian visual and literary traditions. Complicating simplistic ethnographies, her disruption of neo-Orientalist paradigms and representations has led audiences to reconsider Islamophobic, Islamism, and gender repressions that are political, psychological, and above all cross-cultural.

This book will be of interest to scholars working in art history, photography, cinema studies, performance, transnational and global studies, women's studies, and Iranian studies.

Erin Devine is an artist and writer based in Washington, DC and Cologne, Germany. She exhibits installation and performance-based works internationally, contributes criticism to multiple publications, curates exhibitions for spaces in the DC area, and is a Professor of Art History at Northern Virginia Community College.

Routledge Focus on Art History and Visual Studies

Routledge Focus on Art History and Visual Studies presents short-form books on varied topics within the fields of art history and visual studies.

Buckminster Fuller's World Game and Its Legacy
Timothy Stott

Post-Digital Letterpress Printing
Research, Education and Practice
Edited by Pedro Manuel Reis Amado, Ana Catarina Silva and Vítor Quelhas

Bodily Engagements with Film, Images, and Technology
Somavision
Max Ryynänen

Performance, Art and Politics in the African Diaspora
Necropolitics and the Black Body
Myron M. Beasley

Contemporary Art, Systems, and the Aesthetics of Dispersion
Francis Halsall

A Philosophy of Cultural Scenes in Art and Popular Culture
Max Ryynänen and Jozef Kovalčik

Translation and Transgression in the Art of Shirin Neshat
Erin C. Devine

For more information about this series, please visit: https://www.routledge.com/ Routledge-Focus-on-Art-History-and-Visual-Studies/book-series/FOCUSAH

Translation and Transgression in the Art of Shirin Neshat

Erin C. Devine

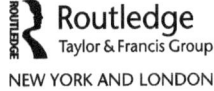
Routledge
Taylor & Francis Group

NEW YORK AND LONDON

First published 2024
by Routledge
605 Third Avenue, New York, NY 10158

and by Routledge
4 Park Square, Milton Park, Abingdon, Oxon, OX14 4RN

Routledge is an imprint of the Taylor & Francis Group, an informa business

ISBN: 9781032376431 (hbk)
ISBN: 9781032376448 (pbk)
ISBN: 9781003341192 (ebk)

DOI: 10.4324/9781003341192

Typeset in Times New Roman
by codeMantra

And we made you into different nations and tribes, so that you may know about each other.

—Qur'an, sura 49:12

Contents

Acknowledgments

I am grateful for the research support of Franklin Furnace Archive, the Fales Library and Special Collections of New York University, and Jeanne Rivoire of the Institut d'Art Contemporain, Villeurbanne/Rhône-Alpes, and the University of Berkeley Art Museum & Pacific Film Archive. I also remain deeply appreciative of the early support I received for this research from Dr. Michelle Facos, Professor of Art History at Indiana University, and the encouragement of colleagues at Northern Virginia Community College, particularly Professor of English LeeAnn Thomas for her invaluable editorial assistance. I must acknowledge that research was made possible by the Lily Fund, and with the support of a Jessie Ball Dupont Research Grant I spent memorable weeks studying the history of Islam at the National Humanities Center. I thank Aliza Edelman and the staff of *Woman's Art Journal* for their publication of a sample of this scholarship, and for their continued dedication to women scholars and artists. I am grateful for the hours of effort and assistance provided by Sarah Willis, Head Archivist at Gladstone Gallery. Finally, I carry profound thankfulness for Editor Isabella Vitti and Editorial Assistant Loredana Zeddita of Routledge Press, without whom this book would not have been realized.

I dedicate this publication to Shirin Neshat and Shoja Azari; the passion and generosity they extend through their work continues to inspire me. I also thank Neshat's studio for their assistance with this project. Lastly and personally, love goes to my husband Jens Goldammer for his support and encouragement throughout this writing, and my friend Dr. Sara Picard, Associate Professor of Art History at Rhode Island College, for her unwavering belief in me all these years.

Introduction

My first encounter with a work by Shirin Neshat was in 1999 at the Art Institute of Chicago. Her video installation *Rapture* (Figure I.1) was featured in its 'Focus' series presenting newly completed works by contemporary artists. I remember walking into the darkened space, encountering two projections of intensely rich, black-and-white imagery. Projected on one wall was the image of a group of men in officious white shirts; on the opposite wall were women in chadors. They looked toward the men, and the men returned their gaze; viewers stood in between, heads bobbing back and forth in anticipation. The projected images offered little specificity aside from what appeared to be a desert setting and Muslim dress. Subtle choreography mitigated a series of actions between the two projected groups: while the men performed exacting yet vague tasks that fused them in a mass within the walls of an old fortress, the women were loosely bound by their sinuous traverse across the landscape.

In the darkened gallery, I stood alongside several other viewers and watched the ten-minute looped film at least twice. Entranced by the rich cinematography and players' mesmerizing movements, our mooring to these synchronized projections seemed an ineffable part of the work's existence, as if without our back-and-forth glances in the darkness, it would disappear. The experience of *Rapture* was profoundly memorable, and I felt compelled to decipher its mysterious references. I found myself wanting to know more especially about the women portrayed. By the time I became aware of the controversies surrounding Neshat's work, it had been several years since I had seen *Rapture*, although I could still recall the hypnotic sound, the chador-clad women, and the pristine tonalities of the black-and-white film. I learned of accusations that she exoticized Muslim female subjects while not taking a firm stand on socio-political issues, particularly following 9/11. Some artists, among them Iranians, accused Neshat of exploiting her culture and appealing to curators in control of international art circuits centralized to West metropolises.[1]

The year 1999 was a watershed in Neshat's career – a woman, a Muslim, an exile. Before the late twentieth-century, it was nearly impossible for an artist fastened to any one of these identifiers to receive such recognition. Neshat would be awarded the First International Prize at the 48th Venice

DOI: 10.4324/9781003341192-1

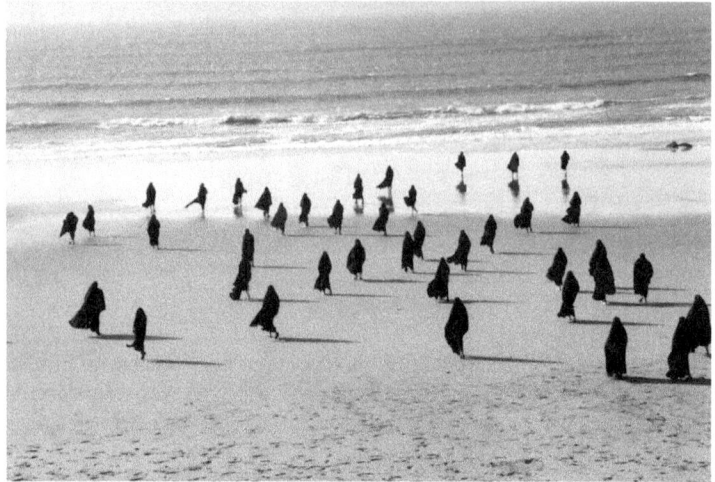

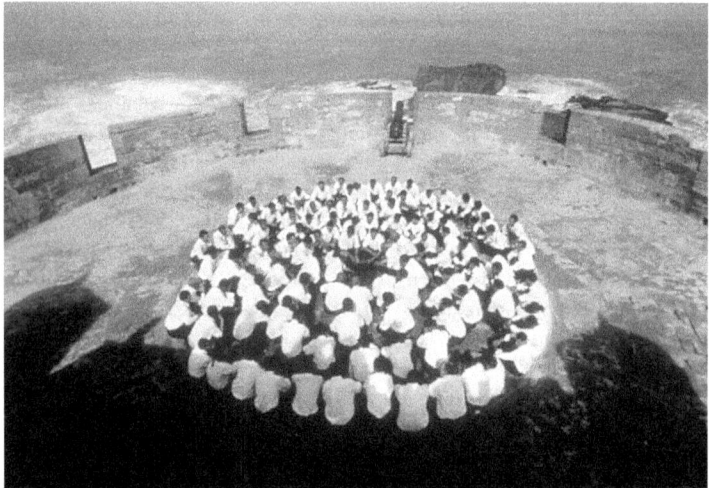

Figure I.1 (a, b) Rapture, 1999. Film Stills, (photos by Larry Barns). © Shirin Neshat. Courtesy of the artist, Gladstone Gallery, and Noirmontartproductions, Paris.

Biennale for another video installation, *Turbulent* (1998). Respected writers like Arthur Danto and Eleanor Heartney praised Neshat's work since she first began exhibiting the photographic series *Women of Allah* (1993–97). Images of Muslim women in chador, often brandishing a Remington rifle or revolver, reinforced images of militant women during the Iranian Revolution, a type portrayed particularly in American media, while they contradicted the image of passivity associated with the veil, a persistent trope of colonialism since the nineteenth-century. Neshat's individual portraits were replete with the contradictions of those competing images, as well as testament to the complexities of any society and its people. These images of a Muslim woman with a gun, often a self-portrait of Neshat, infer a revolutionary subject dedicated to the principles of *jihad* (holy war) while destabilizing their authenticity through performance. Euro-American viewers, unaware of the performative gesture in portrait photography, could reduce the images to representations of terrorism. But the Persian poetry, written across the surface of the photograph and unreadable to those viewers, disrupts oversimplification and enforces a visual barrier that emphasizes translational fissures.

Neshat had pierced two narratives: the passive Muslim female of colonialism and the militant terrorist of neo-colonialism, and she had done so with the adoption of body art and performativity that had been central to Euro-American feminist artists. As a transnational subject, born in Iran and living in the US, Neshat was positioned to create dialog between the two. However, I intuited that her works were far more complex than the binary analyses and claim to an "in-between" or "universality" they often received. I sought to better understand what she intended to translate, only to discover that her translations were hinged upon layers of subtle transgressions, not all apparent to either Iranian viewers or those elsewhere.

My initial impressions of Neshat's work and later knowledge of its debates motivated me to seek answers to basic questions about modern pictorial constructions of Muslim subjectivity, the roots and realities of gender oppressions in Iran. Why was her body of work criticized for opportunistic exoticism, rather than performative evocations that rest upon appropriations of the visual past and present? Why were her videos, lauded for their universality and well-sought under the demands of global exhibition, quickly criticized after 9/11 for that same ambiguity? Beyond the ambiguities and the vacillation between the political and philosophical, was it the sheer pleasure in viewing Neshat's work that was so confounding? Much early feminist art was purposefully void of pleasure, to deny satisfaction of viewing the female body as an aesthetic object. In Neshat's photographs, lines of gestural calligraphy written across an exquisite face create an alluring image; the textures and tonalities of the black-and-white videos of her first trilogy were matched by the vibrant color of the second. The viewer, if trained to recognize pleasure as a trap, may sense a trick: If I enjoy these works, am I the colonizer?

This book addresses these questions and reconsiders the first 20 years of Neshat's career. From 1992 to 2012, Neshat proceeded entirely from Iranian subject matter, further anchoring the work to contemporaneous trends that included an optimism for Internationalism met by the mega-exhibition of biennial culture, the prominence of contemporary art in museum spaces, and the position of transnational artists within these circuits. Neshat's video installations are also important to understanding the cinematic turn within those mega-exhibitions, an absorption of relational aesthetics into a burgeoning era of spectacle. The performativity and embodied practice of her works inter-rogated constructions of identity and adhered closely to feminist art, but her diasporic experience living in the US was largely ignored for the *attribution* of an exotic subject.

It is also important to note the centrality of diasporas to cross-cultural dialog in contemporary art, particularly between what critics and curators labeled "East" and "West." As with the paradigmatic language of Orient/Occi-dent in the past or the Global South/North today, East/West was persistently used, even by Neshat, and pointed to the lingering effects of colonialism and ongoing inequalities under globalization. "East" and "West" perpetuate those effects just as they serve to indicate them, and it is important to note that they will be utilized and addressed at various points throughout these chapters in analyses of global exhibition and the writings that have surrounded Neshat's work. It was framed by claims of "universalism" that transcend East/West, albeit contained within the parameters of a first-world, latent modernity rather than the open praxis of contemporaneity under which globalism is but one element.

Chapter 1 reconsiders Neshat's early photographs, *Unveiling* and *The Women of Allah,* which have been afforded the most scholarship over her career. They were the creative results of three returns to Iran between 1991 and 1995, but also reveal an engagement with multiple visual strategies, the dynamics of portraiture and performativity, and a nuanced understanding of the colonialist gaze. They transgressed many intersecting histories that include women's rights in modern Iran, governmental repression, and the ten-sions between Persian culture and the Islamic state. The poems that Neshat inscribed onto these images are key and recognize the subversive quality of Persian poetry as Iran's most cherished art form; but these images also inflect the theoretical demands of referentiality and representation. Neshat's first solo exhibition, *Unveiling,* contained not only photography but also installation, the latter of which remains ignored. In the first chapter, I revisit these under-recognized aspects of her early career, essential to fully apprehend Neshat's nascent confluences of contemporary practice, Persian folk forms, and modern Iranian art. With support from previous scholarship, most notably by Iftikhar Dadi, Staci Gem Scheiwiller, and Amna Malik, I will trace interpretations of these images. I engage Hamid Keshmirshekan's writings on exoticism to address Neshat's strategic disentanglement of the Muslim female image from its clichés, in essence by complicating them.

Neshat's combined strategies dislodged her images from reductive inter-pretations (although critics still made them). Neshat would carry that strate-gic use of ambiguity into her video installations, described as a "lyricism" more philosophical than political.[2] In **Chapter 2**, I analyze *Anchorage* (1996) and *The Shadow Under the Web* (1997) as transitions toward her first trilogy – *Turbulent, Rapture,* and *Fervor* (2000). With this first trilogy, I will reinvestigate the work's underpinnings to Amelia Jones's intersubjectivity and Raymond Bellour's "cinema-situation," to site their liminality not as an "in-between space" as an end to itself but to achieve Michel Foucault's "limit-experience" as the inflection point for transgression. This theoretical work extends from Neshat's photographs, but her video installations especially drew interest with the contingent appetite for spectacle-experience in large-scale and museum exhibition. The writings of Erika Balsom and Laura Marks also support an understanding of cinema's centrality to art and exhibition.

Neshat's work explicated a broad, humanist understanding of gender; but due to a longstanding propensity to totalize societies under Euro-American circuits of cultural discourse, the descriptive "universal" will be reexamined. To understand global exhibition practices of this period – their divergence from multiculturalism to internationalism and globality – in **Chapter 3** I attempt to unravel the language that attributed Neshat's video installations as "universal" and engage her own adoption of this term. With the debut of her second trilogy – *Pulse, Possessed*, and *Passage* (all 2001) – Neshat sought to underscore humanistic rather than cultural conditions. With support from Caroline Jones, Gerado Mosquera, Homi Bhabha, among others, I will attempt to apprehend the emergence of globality from neocolonial discursive practices, their support for and obstruction to new translatory artistic spaces, informed by indentificatory connections between cosmopolitan, diasporic, exilic, and migrant subjectivities.

Shown in October 2001 at The Kitchen in New York, *Logic of the Birds* was a live performance in the shadow of 9/11, the beginning of an important period for Neshat personally and professionally. Equally allegorical, *Tooba* (2002), her first video after 9/11, was negatively received. Expected to provide a Muslim perspective on 9/11, the universal themes once praised in her work now confounded critics. These criticisms were curiously unconscious of Neshat's precarious position as an exile with family left in Iran. Chapter 3 ends with an autobiographical consideration of *Soliloquy* (1999), an independent work produced between the trilogies that most directly addressed her transnational subjectivity.

Chapter 4 begins with Neshat's *The Last Word* (2003) which both resembled her experience of interrogation at the Tehran airport in 1995 and expressed her admiration for censored Iranian writers. It is a narrative of artistic repression under patriarchal authority and an appropriate transition to Neshat's role as a filmmaker, transgressing both the Iranian regime and the constraints of international contemporary art. *The Last Word* was indicative of her emerging commitment to the political responsibility of artists after 9/11. By the end of the first decade of Neshat's career, she came to embrace the political, choosing to adapt a script for the banned novel, *Women Without Men* (1989) by Shahrnush Parsipur (b. 1946). Its magic realist qualities hinge women's experiences to the backdrop of politics and history. Set during a pivotal period in modern Iran – the US-British sponsored coup d'état of democracy for the restoration of an autocracy – *Women Without Men* afforded Neshat the resolution of central themes across her career: exile, escape, repression of women, oppression by governments, religion and society, Persian culture, modern Iran, and the social and psychological conditions that historically divide "Orient" and "Occident." *Women Without Men* debuted in the wake of Iran's revolutionary Green Movement and profoundly impacted Neshat's status as a social justice artist.

Consciously embracing political activism as moral imperative, her next body of work returned to the photographic portraiture that began her career exactly 20 years prior. Now her subjects were the activists of the Green Movement, embellished with texts by modern Iranian poets and images drawn from Ferdausi's *Shahnama* (ca. 977–1010ce), the epic poem of Persia's pre-Islamic rulers. These photographs provided visual excavations for considering the constructs of power in eras of militaristic expansion from abroad and regime suppression from within. Neshat's *Book of Kings* (2012) serves as a coda to a body of work committed to understanding the psychological effects of patriarchal government repression from the vantage point of one of the world's most complex nations.

Briefly discussed in the **Conclusion**, Neshat's recent public art works recycle her earliest images in response to a new Iranian Revolution contiguous with the writing of this volume. She began work on her most recent exhibition, *The Fury* (2023), in the spring prior to the Woman.Life.Freedom movement, just one example of her prescient sensitivity to historical tides. Across these first two pivotal decades of Neshat's career, these four chapters position her as an artist transgressing the spatial-temporal limitations of identity, history, nation, and gender, and the discourses that attempt to contain her.

Notes

1 Honigman, Ana Finel. "Against the Exotic." *ArtReview* (Sept. 2005). p. 96–99.
2 Azari, Shoja and Shirin Neshat. "In Movement: A Conversation with Shirin Neshat." *Shirin Neshat, 2002–2005*. New York: Charta & Barbara Gladstone Gallery, 2005.

1 Signs in Silence

Performing the Subjects of *Unveiling* and *Women of Allah*

Shirin Neshat's biography is often cursorily abridged in interviews and articles, with limited attention paid to her education in California, or the decade between her move to New York in 1983 and her debut exhibition there in 1993. Writers and interviewers recount that she was born in Iran and left while she was still a teenager to study in the US, where she remained in the wake of the Iranian Revolution. She moved to New York after an MFA from UC-Berkeley and did not return to Iran until 1991. Upon her first return visit, she was shocked by what she saw: the Islamic regime had all but eradicated the Iran of her memory, and she felt for the first time that she had something to say through art.

In truth, Neshat felt compelled toward an interrogatory project addressing the changes in her homeland since her absence. However, the emphasis upon her first return home in 1991 as the genesis of her work ignores its transnational influences to favor a discourse of otherness. Rather, the troubling experience of witnessing her culture's transformation through the lens of its primary adversary would also impact her work. As the Iranian Revolution (1978–79) unfolded via the American media, she was quite young and isolated: "By the time I got to Berkeley, the Revolution happened, and I was caught off guard. The borders closed and I had to support myself. There was no communication with Iran."[1] In addition to this isolation, she felt circumspect as a young Iranian student during the hostage of the American Embassy in Tehran (1979–81). Anti-Iran protests escalated at Berkeley and around the country while many students returning to Iran were killed under the new regime.

Neshat was born in Qazvin, near the northwest border of Iran and the Caspian Sea. Her father was a physician who had supported Mohammad Reza Shah Pahlavi and the generally pro-Western political agenda the monarch established in Iran, in no small part because his reign had been backed by an American-British sponsored coup-d'état in 1953. Many upper-class Iranians sent their children abroad in Europe or America for their education and, in December 1973 at the age of sixteen, Neshat was sent with an older sister

DOI: 10.4324/9781003341192-2

to Los Angeles where they lived in a modest apartment subsidized by their parents. Neshat's sister returned to Iran, and after high school she worked as a nanny before moving to San Francisco to live with relatives. Without her immediate family or fluency in English, Neshat described these early years as a period of loneliness and isolation. Eventually however, she was drawn to the Northern California landscape and persevered to complete her education there. She enrolled in Dominican College, a Catholic liberal arts school in San Rafael, regardless that her previous parochial education in a strict, Tehrani boarding school had left her both anxious and anorexic.[2] In 1979, she transferred to UC-Berkeley to pursue a degree in art. These formative experiences – her fortitude to remain virtually alone in San Francisco, a strong connection to the surrounding landscape, and a profound bodily reaction to a strict surroundings – undergird a creative attentiveness toward the effects of environment both physically and psychologically.

This period of separation from her home and family, intensely marked by revolution and war, lasted until 1991 when Neshat made her first return to Iran since 1977 – just before revolution broke out and prior to Ayatollah Ruhollah Khomeini's rise to power over the new Islamic Republic of Iran (IRI). With the end of the Iran-Iraq War (1980–88), the death of Khomeini in 1989, and her US citizenship in 1986, Neshat and her family agreed it was safe for her to visit without jeopardizing her return to New York, where she then lived with a husband and infant son. Taking advantage of relaxed laws permitting diasporic citizens to reenter the country, she made three visits between 1991 and 1995. Witnessing firsthand the nation that had replaced the Iran of her memory, she translated her profound visual experiences into the series *Unveiling* (1992–93) and *Women of Allah* (1993–97).

Neshat's transnational perspective to the development of these photographs relied upon the portrait-mode in their re-presentation of identity. In the fusion of text to image, a subversion is extended but obscured by a screen of calligraphy across the female body, both conceptually and formally abstract, inviting further layers of interpretation. Ultimately, the images challenge colonialist and neo-colonialist visualities, destabilizing assumptions of Muslim identity generally and Iranian women particularly. They encourage, and even necessitate, consideration of the texts' translations and knowledge of Iran's vacillating enforcements regarding *hijab* (modest dress) in the twentieth century, beginning with the Unveiling Act (1936) and later the Veiling Act (1983). Fueled by modernization and desecularization respectively, these subjugating laws rendered the female body as cultural marker of the nation-state. Neshat's photographs will rely upon and resist reductive significations of exoticized subjects, affixing them to complexities that compel viewers to look beyond first glance.

The Double-Consciousness of Diaspora

By the time of her annual visits, Neshat's knowledge of the political and identificatory issues the veil encompassed were further complicated by the American media's representations of revolutionary Iranian women. Images that have circulated in Western media since Iran's Revolution emphasized the chador as a sign of otherness, disturbing for viewers who were shocked by the violence inflicted on women and outraged by the militancy of women bearing arms, crying 'death to America.' Neshat could appear to have placated viewers who fail to understand the complexity of social and religious identity in Iran or the diversity of women's experiences there. Such audiences could read these photographs as either a feminist indictment of Iranian/Islamic society or conversely an endorsement of terrorism. Neshat adopted performativity to strategically enact alterities and the instability of identity in photographs that were a complex response to contradictory images of passivity and violence. Exploiting the documentary nature of photography, she subverted control from the Western imaginary of veiled women, exposing the limitations of its visual contexts for Muslim female subjects. In an indictment of both Iran and the US, each exploiting the veiled female body as cultural sign, she reclaims the veil from its politicized agendas and delivers it to multi-faceted and ambiguous meanings.

Cut off from her family, at UC-Berkeley she was a struggling student making what she referred to as "mediocre art." Her "ideas were confused and simply not strong enough" and she "wasn't really inspired by the art history."[3] Whatever that curriculum included in the early 1980s, it did not aid Neshat to fully explore her interests or develop a convincing body of work addressing her diasporic experience. Now known for photography, video, and film, Neshat's degree was in painting. Although there are no images of Neshat's early work, much of which she destroyed,[4] her submission to the MFA exhibition at the Berkeley Art Museum in 1982 included four untitled works of moderate size (34×46 inches) whose media included house paint, watercolor, pastel, and collage. This accumulation of materials perhaps bears tendencies of Neo-Expressionist painting in the early 1980s, particularly multi-media abstraction. The exhibition, *Twenty-Nine Degrees*, named for the twenty-nine participating graduates, was reviewed by fellow student Andrea Sadeghi for the campus newspaper, *The Daily California*:

> Shirin Neshat's four untitled collages are delicate, ghostly depictions of vacant rooms, with doors leading to other rooms. Figures of women, rather like suffering Madonnas in their sorrowful attitudes, fade into pastel shades, through doorways and coffin-like boxes. The doorways, walls, boxes -- all are drawn with complete reserve, yet they conspired to suggest fully dimensional rooms and other rooms beyond.[5]

Even without surviving images, it is still plausible to imagine the "suffering Madonnas" as veiled women. Media images of the unrest in Iran and the Iran Hostage Crisis had dominated the news, and the impending Veiling Act, certainly filled her mind. In a hand-written biography that accompanied her thesis statement, Neshat's vulnerable disclosure revealed her loneliness, but also her independent spirit in the phrase "relocated myself to Northern California."[6] Even then, Neshat's struggle with the circumstances and restrictions of exile, the double-consciousness of being both the observer and the observed, manifest in an imagery of women who also seemed suspended within ambiguous spaces. As revealed in Neshat's artist statement, an interest in the bodily experience of environments, explored profoundly in her later video work, is even apparent in these lost paintings.

Her bravery and independence also led her to move to New York the following year, when painting was a dominant medium in an inflated art market. Yet as a young artist, she felt intimidated and overwhelmed.[7] In her first years, she worked as a receptionist, then as a designer for a textile company until she arrived at The Storefront for Art & Architecture in 1985. For the next ten years, she performed a wide range of duties, everything from cleaning to assisting with the curatorial program and eventually marrying founder Kyong Park. Located in Lower Manhattan, The Storefront is an experimental incubator for architects, artists, curators, and critics. Its well-known projects during Neshat's tenure included an inaugural program on performance and *After Tilted Arc*, an exhibition about the controversial removal of Richard Serra's *Tilted Arc* from New York's Federal Plaza. It included contributions by and discussions with Carolee Schneemann, Mierle Laderman Uekles, Hannah Wilke, and Nancy Spero. Additional artists with whom Neshat interacted during her tenure included Vito Acconci, Kiki Smith, and Jenny Holzer. In the words of Neshat, this is where her true education occurred, where she "began to develop [her] own ideas and methodology."[8] But her artistic output was reduced to a few group exhibitions between 1985 and 1992, immersing herself into the collaborative programs The Storefront showcased.

Returning to Iran, Neshat was both "shocked" and "exhilarated" because she "had never seen a society in which everyone functioned under a common ideology."[9] The new regime was eager to eradicate and replace any vestige of "Westoxication," the corruption of Iranian society by consumerism and economic dependence on the West, and she was frightened by an Iran that was no longer like anything she remembered. The transformation Iran had undertaken and Neshat now witnessed influenced her "to create a group of works that somehow could convey my emotions, my responses, and my understanding of the profound political changes."[10] Prior to her first gallery representation in 1995, she was free to make work without preconceived expectations. Stark black-and-white images appeared straightforward, even confrontational; but an emotive exploration drove the content, particularly in images of Neshat herself. These self-portraits masqueraded an experience of chador as an interstitial engagement through travel and return, underscoring the images as performative excavations toward that understanding. This only underscores the images as performative, and the textual markings on the body are also significant to the performative gesture. In performing, she will later attempt to understand women's militant participation in an oppressive state as well as complicate their ascribed meaning as visual signs.

Unveiling

Following her first visit to Iran in May 1991, Neshat was granted a residency at Henry Street Settlement and took two days away from The Storefront each week to contemplate and experiment. She moved from drawing to eventually writing Persian poems onto Xerox copies of photographs. Within two years of her first visit home, she responded to a call for proposals for emerging performance artists from the experimental non-profit, Franklin Furnace, then located in Lower Manhattan. There in April 1993, Neshat's first series *Unveiling* was shown as a solo exhibition. These self-portraits of Neshat and images of her eyes, feet, and hands – the only parts of the female body publicly visible under Iran's restrictive dress code – were first presented as unmatted 8×10-inch prints under glass (Figure 1.1). Although untrained in photography, Neshat recognized the medium's centrality to the performative portrait in offering new constructs of alterity and identity among contemporary artists.[11] Across both the *Unveiling* and *Women of Allah* series, she gathered the assistance of photographers Plauto, Cynthia Preston, Bahman Jalali, and Larry Barns to execute and print the new images she conceived. She would stage the compositions in the studio, make decisions regarding lighting and printing, and undertake the painterly calligraphy onto the completed photos before they were then rephotographed.

Traveling to and from Iran, the depictions of the veiled woman Neshat created helped her to process a drastically changed homeland, while the images relied upon and questioned the divergent implications of veiling for different audiences. Yet this first iteration of *Unveiling* included installation elements and sculptural references to Iranian folk art, such as talismanic plates in the shape of a hand. Neshat had collected such hand-shaped artifacts in Tehrani bazaars, some of which contain human and animal forms that have been covered with inscriptions.[12] The projected eye in Super-8 film onto a large, hand-shaped metal plate, represented the Eye of Fatimah, the daughter of Mohammad and one of few female saints recognized in Islam. Other hands appeared surrounded by rocks and encased under glass, like archaeological excavations of the past on display (Figure 1.2). More broadly

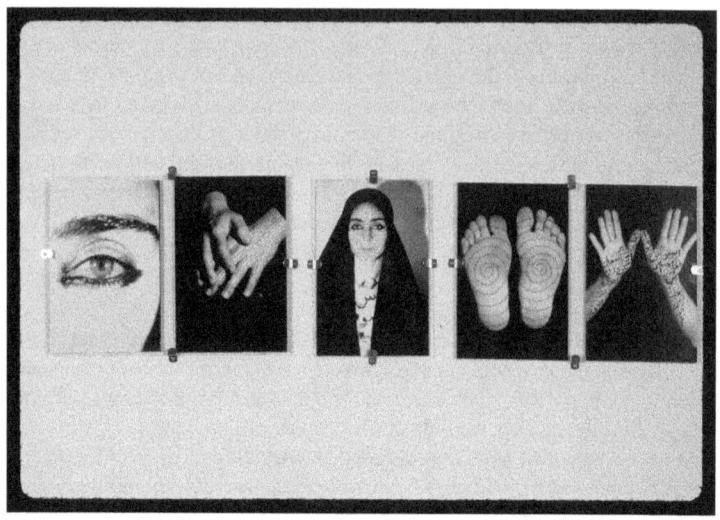

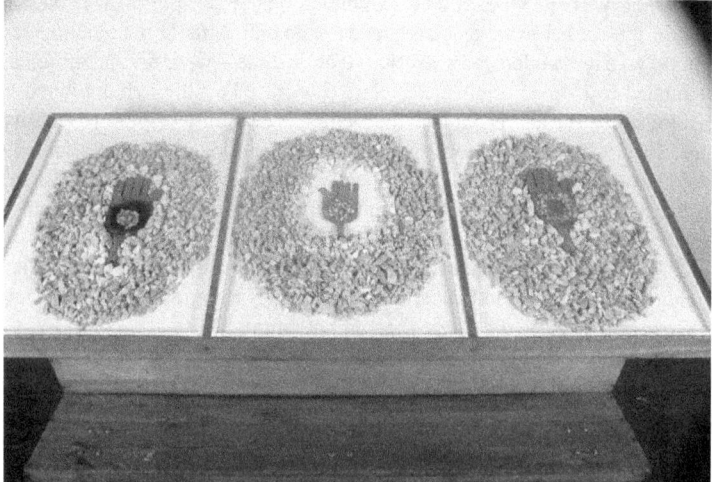

Figures 1.1 and 1.2 Unveiling, 1993. Installation photos by Marty Heitner. © Shirin Neshat. Courtesy Franklin Furnace Archive.

known throughout Middle Eastern cultures as the *hamsa*, the amulet of a hand with an eye at its center traces back to ancient Mesopotamia and was a sign of good luck and protection from evil. In Iran, they also reference the severed hands of Shi'i martyrs who attempted to bring water from the Euphrates to Imam Hossein and his followers. Detained at the Battle of Karbala in the late seventh-century, it is one of the defining historical breaks between Shi'i and Sunni Muslims.

In this debut exhibition, the collusion of installation and sculptural elements based on national folk-objects potentially signify "recollection-objects...the cracks in material reality in which one can read repressed histories."[13] Encased as fossil and appropriated within the installation, Neshat imbues these objects and portrait-subjects equally with significance and history. Thus, her early representations of Iranian women alongside these installations suggest an already/always-codified body, entwined within a broader complex of nationalist identifications, cultural tradition, and political forces that contradictorily celebrate and violently repress women. The most overtly political gesture was the Super-8 projection of the shadow of a recumbent woman onto an installation of rocks called *Stoned Carpet*. In Islam, the stone is a mediator between the human in the act of prayer and their connection with the eternal or divine through the *mohr* (praying stone) that Muslims touch or bow upon. But in her original proposal to Franklin Furnace, Neshat's reference to a "stoned body" co-signifies religion's violence.[14] Conceptually replacing the material knots of the Persian carpet with stones, Neshat signaled the replacement of Persian art traditions viewed as minor or even irrelevant under the Islamic regime, therefore asserting that censorship of art and objects, and the restrictions and violence imposed upon the female body, are causally related, put forth as they are by the same repressive forces of religion and government.

With *Unveiling*, Neshat established hallmarks of her practice in the fusion of text and image and the appropriation of Persian and Islamic material culture. It was the Saqqakhaneh artists, the first cohesively recognizable modernist art movement in Iran, that first incorporated a specifically Persian formal rhetoric. Coined by a critic in 1962 to describe a group of artists in Tehran who were interested in Iranian folk art, they were so-called for the repeated visual references in their paintings and sculpture to the Saqqakhaneh, a public drinking fountain often with the image of a hand installed in wall niches and dedicated to the early Shi'ite martyrs at the Battle of Karbala. The Saqqakhaneh artists, or "spiritual pop artists," who felt reverence for iconic objects of Iranian-Islamic tradition, also incorporated calligraphy, not only for its abstract embellishment but its historical and sacred associations. Armed with the visual and the verbal, they capitalized on calligraphy's potential abstraction and the multiple meanings of Persian poetry and language. This provided them with a stylistic visual marker as well as multiple indicators of political resistance, combining the gestural lines of calligraphy into works that were contiguous with Minimalism, Pop, and abstraction.

Neshat also appropriated traditional Islamic and Persian art, bringing them under modes of contemporary practice she had been exposed to in New York. The Franklin Furnace exhibition marked the beginning of Neshat's creative reliance upon multiple transcultural influences. She will later describe her photographic series as "minimalist, sculptural, rigid [like] carved monuments,"[15] indicating a process conceptually steeped in an architectural understanding of the body's relationship to space, evident in her earliest paintings and reinforced by her time at The Storefront. Juxtaposing multiple underlying practices and meanings, such as bodily projections upon inanimate steel and stone surfaces, the low-brow folk traditions of the religious Saqqakhaneh or the magical hamsa, and the high-brow art of carpet-weaving, each construct the past and present of Iran. Where her Saqqakhaneh predecessors blamed cultural suppression on a brutally intimidating monarchy, Neshat saw the same loss of culture under the censorship of an Islamist government. In Neshat's usage, folk art and poetry are materials for resisting the dissipation of Persian culture under the Islamic Republic. Saqqakhaneh artists adapted similar cultural references in response to the West-centric modernization of the Pahlavi period. Their malaise and disillusionment were often reflected in calligraphic appropriation as abstraction, escaping "the futility of the search for meaning in words, seeking solace in the abstract shapes of letters" and "restat[ing] the importance of the written word as a form that is open to multiple interpretations."[16] Calligraphy, Persian poetry, and Shi'ite folk art were symbolic of a culture under threat for these artists; however, Neshat's approach differed in that the female body was centrally positioned as the barometer of cultural and political shifts. Just as the body provides multiple performativities, the art of poetry and calligraphy, as adopted into works by Muslim artists from the Saqqakhaneh to Neshat, denotes multiple strategies.

Bodies Written and Silent

Inscribed on skin against the clinging chador is an incomprehensible calligraphy; illegible to most viewers in the context of a Lower Manhattan art gallery, it is a message extended but lost in translatory suspense. The Persian poetry, written in the Arabic calligraphy, culminates both verbal and visual expression and the potential for multiple revolutionary forms via the written word, even if the subject is silent and the language unfamiliar. The multiple meanings of words and turns of phrases provided a means by which Iranian writers could subvert political authority and censorship. Yet writing is also a symbolic projection of action, and here the body further bears the burden of a textual meaning inextricable from corporeal experience. Non-Muslim viewers could assume the texts are derived from the Qur'an based on the Arabic calligraphy and its status as an Islamic art form. Tied to the sacred act of rewriting and recitation, the veiled body is equally imbricated as Islamic symbol in the West. Regardless of "meaning," it is significant that she functions as a bearer of meaning, the surface upon which the texts are written. Investigating Neshat's resolution of both Orientalism and Modernism, Amna Malik emphasized process, stating that the inscribed images, rephotographed to fuse the ink seamlessly and permanently with the emulsion, symbolically seals together the Muslim subjects and the texts.[17] In the mode of either classic self-portrait or the contemporary practice of performative self-display, Neshat is both the surface upon which the text lies and the absent body that writes it. Therefore, Neshat's act of writing is as performative as putting on a chador and posing for the camera.

Though both series bear inscriptions of Persian texts onto women in chador, there were essential differences between *Unveiling* and *Women of Allah*. *Unveiling* presents Orientalized tropes of seduction with poetry by Forough Farrokhzad (1935–67). In *Women of Allah*, the artist brandishes a rifle and pistol, a recollection of revolution and the Iran-Iraq War in which many women participated. Much of these date to 1994 and are inscribed with the poems of Tahereh Saffarzadeh (1936–2008), who espoused revolutionary virtues upheld by Khomeini. From 1995, Neshat retained the veil within her visual vocabulary but largely withdrew from overt militant iconography, expanding images to include self-portraits with her son (1995–96), group-portraits of women in Iran (1996), and closely cropped double-portraits of a man and woman (1997). In these later iterations, texts were expanded to include writings by the novelist Moniru Ravani'pur (b. 1954) and poet Simin Behbahani (1927–2014). Before the conclusion of *Women of Allah*, Neshat returns to Farrokhzad poems that, alongside Saffarzadeh, comprise most of the texts, and the two poets are sharply contradictory.

Farrokhzad is known for the sensuality and eroticism of her categorically feminist poems, and Saffarzadeh for a religious fervor and reverence for martyrdom. Transcribed by Neshat onto the surfaces of the photographs, their divergent content underscores her awareness of the dichotomies that underlie the lived experiences of women in Iran. The gesture of their inclusion is subversive to a viewpoint that these images of veiled Muslim subjects are mysterious and erotic in *Unveiling*, or hostile and terroristic in *Women of Allah,* or an assumption that the texts come from the Qur'an. A spiritual emphasis is placed upon recitation through writing of the Qur'an, and thereby the poetry of Farrokhzad and Saffarzadeh are imbued with a sacred import when transcribed, especially in Neshat's repetition of two central poems: Farrokhzad's *I Pity the Garden* (also *I Feel Sorry for the Garden*) and Saffarzadeh's *Allegiance with Wakefulness*. Both poems reveal revolutionary sentiment, expressed as political disillusionment by Farrokhzad and religious and patriotic faith by Saffarzadeh. The excerpt of *I Pity the Garden* that appears on the white of Neshat's eye in *Offered Eyes* (Figure 1.1) reads:

> no one is thinking about the flowers no one is thinking about the fish
> no one wants to believe that the garden is dying
> that the garden's heart has swollen under the sun that the garden
> is slowly forgetting its green moments
> [translated from image, Nasim Moadab]

A translator of Farrokhzad's work, Farzaneh Milani prefers "the garden is slowly forgetting its green moments" rather than an alternative translation, "the garden's mind is slowly being drained of green memories"[18] Yet the personification of a garden with a 'mind' capable of thought and memory extends the metaphor to Iran and its people. The garden also becomes a space in time whose people are conflicted and divided as they struggle to move forward.

Farrokhzad's poem conveys a range of attitudes toward the garden's neglect – from the patriarch who turns his back on it to the mother who sees its decay as a direct result of sin. Continuing with Milani's translation, their son, who holds the future of industry, appears to be as callous as his father, believing that the garden's cure "lies in its destruction." Finally, his sister who was "the flowers' friend" lives in "an artificial home singing artificial songs," while producing "very real babies." Farrokhzad places the greatest responsibility with the young woman who, once the most closely connected with the world of nature, has betrayed the garden by concurring with the gendered roles of a society that allowed the garden to fall into ruin. As for the narrator of the poem, her feelings are summarized toward the poem's end:

> I fear an age
> that has lost its heart.
> I am scared of the thought of so many useless hands

Farrokhzad's assessment of her era, torn between culture and modernity, was written when Mohammad Reza Shah was enabling capitalist Imperialism through a close relationship with the US. It is bitingly sharp, expressing frustration with her fellow citizens' apathy. Neshat's inscription on the white of her own eye in *Offered Eyes,* positions herself as witness and the viewer as reflexive co-witness to the society the poet confronts.

Farrokhzad's rise as a highly regarded poet occurred in the 1950s and 1960s alongside major shifts in Iranian art and politics. Her education as a child was surprisingly limited for such an accomplished writer, though typical at a time when percentages of boys and girls attending and completing school remained low in Iran until the 1960s. She married young and following her divorce custody of her only child went to the father's family. Still, she pursued a highly autobiographical poetry with an openness and intimacy about her experiences as a woman seeking love, sex, autonomy, and a life dedicated to her own art – expressions and perspectives daring for a woman in virtually any country in that period. Farrokhzad's poetry also coincides the complex shifts of her society, in which Mohammad Reza Shah gradually introduced reforms that included marriage, divorce, and custody rights, as well as equal access to education and positions of high office. Published in 1963, the same year women gained voting rights, *I Feel Sorry for the Garden* broadly thematized the repression of self-individuation viewed as unconventional but could be more specifically interpreted as a critique of American dependency and a regime that censored media and brutally suppressed dissent. Farrokhzad today is regarded as one of the modern Iranian poets who contributed a nationalist vision opposing the restrictive intimidation under Pahlavi.

Farrokhzad and Saffarzadeh represent and reflect on the paradoxical situation of the lives of women in Iran. Both opposed the intrusion of what they saw as Western Imperialism; but while Farrokhzad's concern with class distinction under the Shah could be categorized as nationalist, Saffarzadeh's anti-Imperialism is expressly Islamist. Like Neshat and many Iranians of the Pahlavi era, she moved to the US, enrolling into the University of Iowa's acclaimed Creative Writing program in 1963, becoming a recognized translator of Persian and English texts. The subjects of her poetry – death, love, revenge, and the weight of history – have led critics to classify her work also as universal. It may have been this approach that appealed to Neshat, whose own work used the cultural situation of Iran to explore broadly humanist themes. Saffarzadeh returned to Iran in the late 1970s to become a supporter of Khomeini and the revolution. While Farrokhzad decried the repression and limitations placed upon women, Saffarzadeh upheld traditional Islamic values that advocated strict male/female roles as interpreted from the Qur'an; but her poetry petitioned equal participation in defense of the nation as a right of all devout Muslims.

Neshat seems to exploit the pleasure of looking with the earlier series *Unveiling,* in the projected eye onto the metal hand or the centrality of the eye in the photographs of *Offered Eyes* and *I Am Its Secret.* The exaggerative signs of the seductive Oriental are subverted by a text that obscures the meaning of the subject's outward gaze toward the viewer while extending a lost, verbal translation. While these rely upon seduction and prescriptive femininity, they also emphasize the scopophilia inherent to surveilling, witnessing, and viewing. Neshat utilized preconceived images of femininity as a transgressive performance that emphasizes the body as the center of discourse, appropriator of language, and bearer of meaning, although for these subjects the emphasis upon looking emphatically positions them alternately as the empowered and censored subject of the gaze.

By the 1990s, the use of text had emerged from Conceptual through Feminist Art to a pluralist strategy of identity and social practice among artists like Xu Bing, Ann Hamilton, Glenn Ligon, and Carrie Mae Weems. With the female body serving as the poem's page, Neshat demarcates the barriers between subject and viewer, between presumed knowledge and understanding. Within this "gap" between access and denial to the subject, the viewer may become aware of their own malleability. Writers such as Luce Irigaray, Trinh T. Minh-ha, and Gloria Anzaldúa have addressed the transgressive act of writing as a strategy of resistance to dominant forms of language, one that can provide a path toward self-mastery. A woman's transcription of the words of women challenges the dominant discourses traditionally inscribed onto the female body. Translation reveals another layer of meaning to Neshat's photos, and through her handwriting recitation emphasizes replacement of Qur'anic verse and even mosque decoration, inferring these bodies as sacred and cultural sites. But interpretation is made further complex by the layered meanings of poetry and the subject-position of these specific writers. Equitable to the fragmented experiences of Farrokhzad and Saffarzadeh, such destabilization denies a monolithic identity easily translated. In Staci Gem Scheiwiller's astute readings of these surfaces, she notes that even for readers of Persian the texts are fragmented because Neshat's writing itself records pieces of the poems and repetitive excerpts further disrupted by the irregularities of curves and contours of the bodies onto which they are transcribed.[19]

Malik observed the fusing of body and text is the creation of a new language and Ann Rosalind Jones has stated that "to write from the body is to recreate the world."[20] The subject of *I Am Its Secret* enunciates a new capacity for love as power as indicated by the inscribed poem while "It" is left unclear. The poem spirals from a point between her large, heavily made-up eyes, peering out from the veil. Neshat reinscribed Farrokhzad's *I Will Greet the Sun Again*, whose speaker is "replete with love" and will be defiantly "waiting for those who love." A different style of language to create a different world recalls the "écriture feminine" of Hélène Cixous. Similarly, Neshat's photographs resist patriarchal language not only in the adoption of women's words but their inscription onto bodies recodes the cultural and psychological readings they have been forced to bear. This hermeneutic approach reinterprets text as symbolically fused to the body and, according to this interpretive model, the word and the veil are inseparable from the female body under the Islamist regime.

As introduced earlier, writing on the bodies inscribes the expressions of women writers as an inherently crucial aspect of the works' performativity, transgressing the dominance of patriarchy across cultures that politicize women's bodies visually and textually. Iranian women, epitomized by Farrokhzad and Saffarzadeh, seemed to "divide into two distinct groups: those who are bitterly resentful of the Islamic codes, and others who are living at ease and fully support the Islamic regime."[21] These contradictory positions raise important questions about traditional Islam and the role of women within it. Neshat's return to art began as a personal working-through of these matters after her in-person witness to them. Absent for the revolution that traumatized and transformed Iran, she responded by becoming "obsessed with an understanding of the roots and causes of these changes, and with finding ways to once again feel a part of this community."[22] Her transnational perspective enabled clear detection of the paradoxes for women living there, while indicating the limited understanding of these women in the US.

The Women of Allah

Neshat experienced living with veil enforcement for herself on her first visit to Iran in 1991. A faction of the police, the Gasht-e Ershad (Guidance Patrol) monitored city streets to ensure that women adhered to the dress code's tenets: only hands, feet, and face exposed, without make-up or nail polish. Any woman defying the code, or taking liberty with it, could be fined, detained, or imprisoned. The *Women of Allah* series presented a detectable shift from *Unveiling*, from the emphasis on the private space of women's bodies, overlaid with poems by Farrokhzad, to their radical participation in political revolution with poems by Saffarzadeh. As Neshat's visits to Iran continued, her focus shifted from dress code tenets to militant activism, from silence to defiance, transgressing the spectatorial power of Western viewers and Islamic patriarchal authority.

After the Franklin Furnace exhibition and throughout 1994, Neshat was staging powerful depictions of armed women who, despite their participation in the Revolution, experienced severe restriction and inequality. Alternating melancholy and defiance underlie the images despite their intimidating force. The still nature of the photograph captures a silence further evident in the titles and the muffling of voices behind the strident presence of weapons. An early transitional image into this series, *Faceless*, presented Neshat in performance as an empowered Muslim woman in traditional clothes, facing the viewer with bold eyes although her mouth is erased by the pistol she bears. In works such as *Rebellious Silence* (Figure 1.3), Neshat brandishes a Remington rifle used in the Iran-Iraq War. She stares out from the confines of the frame, assailing the viewer's gaze and arresting their removed position as spectator. The directness of her gaze and the frontality of her position defy Islamic tenets of female modesty. Yet the barrel of the rifle dividing her face closes her lips to speech.

In *Speechless* (Figure 1.4), the text is a formal address to "brothers and sisters" after the revolution, both mourning and celebrating its martyrs. A longer excerpt from the poem is written on the closely cropped face to the right of the rifle barrel. Covering the woman's skin, the script recedes her face from the viewer. In many photos of the series, the script reveals the flatness of the 2-d surface, obfuscating the depths and contours of the face that installs a screen-like division between viewer and viewed, the interiority of the subject left impenetrable. This emphasis on flatness rests somewhat within modernist constraints, entangling the surface elements and subject. Saffarzadeh's poem, *Allegiance with Wakefulness* (1980), is altered by its intimate relationship with the surface of the female's face, its contours disappear into the veil, signifying the revocation of rights for even women who fight alongside men. The forces of patriarchy are so encoded that the woman's resistance is accompanied by a sense of imminent physical and psychological threat emphasized by the barrel of the gun, dangerously near her face.

In the photographic image of the same title, an excerpt of the poem appears on the soles of Neshat's feet, held together to balance the barrel of a rifle and form the focal point of the image. Yet the frame also exposes a forbidden ankle and blurred in the background a bare left arm steadying the rifle. In each of these images, the body is the site from which action and information arise

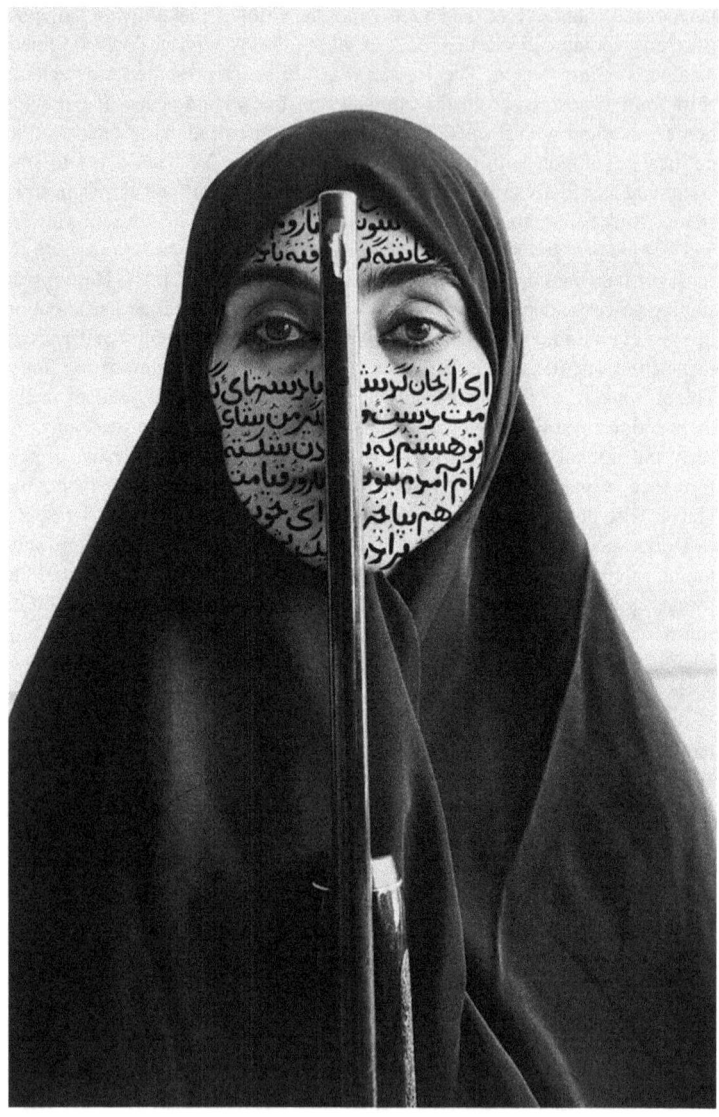

Figure 1.3 Rebellious Silence, 1994. RC print & ink (photo by Cynthia Preston). 46 5/8×43 3/4 inches (118.4×111.1 cm). © Shirin Neshat. Courtesy the artist and Gladstone Gallery.

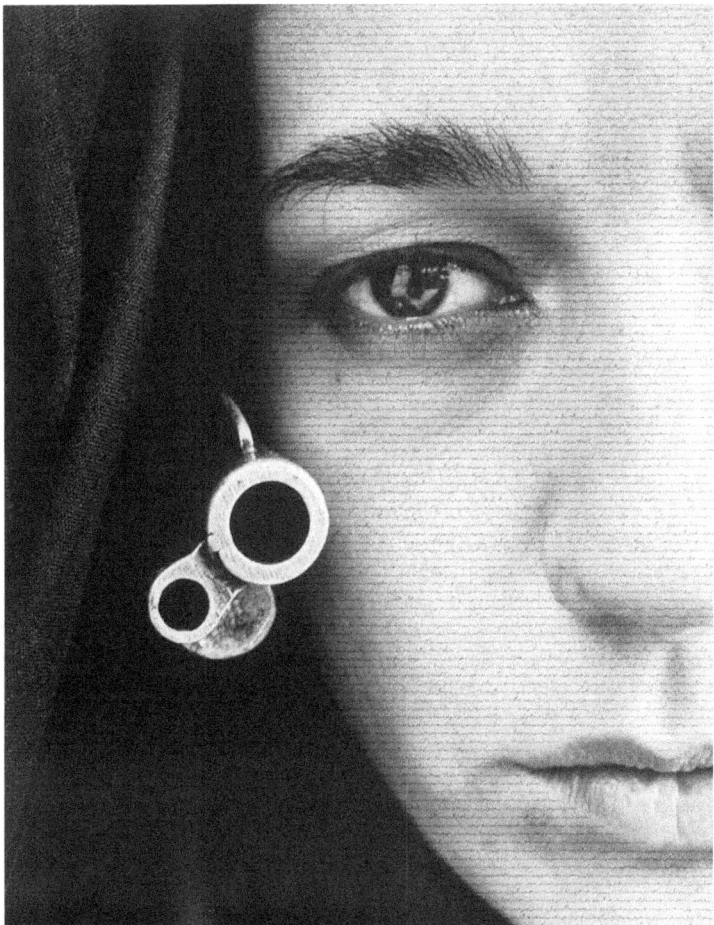

Figure 1.4 Speechless 1996. RC print & ink. 46 3/4×33 7/8 inches (118.7×86 cm).
© Shirin Neshat. Courtesy the artist and Gladstone Gallery.

and thus envelops the pictorial space. The recurrence of Saffarzadeh's poem alongside the weapons urges a reading of the veil's resistance to the Pahlavi regime rather than Western feminist critique.

O, you martyr
hold my hands

with your hands
cut from earthly means,
Hold my hands,
I am your poet,
With an inflicted body,
I've come to be with you
and on the promised day
we shall rise again.

With her "inflicted body," the narrator speaks of herself as an imperfect being (not male) and can only hope that by recording the heroism of others, she may also rise to glory in the afterlife. In presenting Saffarzadeh's admiration for the martyrs of the revolution, the "brother" invoking the comradeship of militant struggle, and in the poetic cadence of "hands cut" the original martyred brothers at Karbala. Neshat's photos are suggestive of an admiration for women who fought in the Iran-Iraq War, and for those before who hoped to "rise again" to claim a higher position within the *ummah* (Muslim community) denied to them on earth.

Although Saffarzadeh's poem celebrates the Islamic tenets of *shahaadat* (martyrdom), it also confirms the political situation of Iranian women who were encouraged to fight in times of war and revolution yet were legally repressed in the nation they supported. Here, shahaadat is an expression of courage rather than the manifestation of fanaticism often represented in the US. Therefore, Neshat simultaneously constructs an image of courage and an image of threat based on the cultural viewpoint of the spectator. As Neshat observed, "Whether or not you agree that it is right or wrong it is [martyrdom] a great sense of devotion" and that "in a way, they are good people because they are so willing to sacrifice themselves in the name of the community and their faith."[23] Neshat has since stated her conflicted viewpoints on this early work, insisting that her interest in revolutionaries in the *Women of Allah* should not be construed as condoning martyrdom but as offering a new dimension of the "terrorist" as someone who follows to their death what they believe to be a moral imperative. Later, she reflected that the series may have offered a romanticized view of women in revolutionary society.[24]

In 1995, Neshat introduced portrait subjects she had photographed during her last visit to Tehran. There she met Bahman Jalali, founder of Iran's first museum for photography and an instructor at many universities. With his assistance, she created highly staged compositions reminiscent of early Orientalist studio photographs, some featuring groups of women rather than a single subject. The images made with Jalali parody colonialist fantasies and Qajar photos, relying upon the exportation of erroneous images to curious Europeans. The studio backdrop of the titular *Women of Allah* is suggestive of those nineteenth-century photographic studios in Near East countries, which largely exoticized Muslim women for Western consumption. But such images of women were also consumed within Iran, whose tastes remarkably resembled those of foreign audiences, cultivated under the tutelage of early photographic innovators in Europe. Three years after the release of Daguerre's 1839 patent by the French government, the first camera arrived in the Qajar court as a gift from Queen Victoria, then another from Tsar Nicholas I (certainly a sign of Imperial powers' colonial thirst for the region). Photography quickly developed both within and outside the court, with many professional photographers going abroad to purchase equipment and learn techniques. With a garden and portico as the simulated backdrop, Neshat consciously adopted staging of those images, upending their reliability as a record of the private realm of women. In their parody, her "garden pictures" replicate colonialist desire for a romanticized and exotic Orientalism, whereas the constructed performativity inherent to the more militant *Women of Allah* images aligned neo-colonialism with multicultural desires for difference. If Neshat's work can be interpreted as perpetuating the contradictory stereotypes of gun-toting revolutionaries and subjugated women, that is exactly the point: the viewer is made more aware of these prejudicial comprehensions and limited visual references.

Exhibition as Liminality

Neshat's photos compel viewers to contemplate not only assumptions of the modern Islamic world but their own social positioning under patriarchal systems. In comprehending the stranger before them, the viewer confronts comparative ideological systems of coded values and consequential rules. Particularly in Western Europe, the veil has long symbolized erotic sensuality and the mysterious exoticism of a highly sexualized Other that serves men's fantasies. In the waning years of Imperial sovereignty, the veil also symbolized a strange and threatening resistance: the dangerous Other of revolution. Women in Iran have also contended with the veil's multiple meanings that change based on local traditions and class associations, and waver between religious identity and the struggle for national self-determination.

Neshat's first exhibition was contemporaneous with the 1993 Whitney Biennial, a watershed exhibition in late twentieth-century art. The exhibition stirred up much controversy, perhaps more than director David Ross and head curator Elisabeth Sussman anticipated, although it did not seem to introduce anything radically different from what had been standard fare in contemporary exhibition practices since the 1980s. As Hal Foster summarized in a panel response to the exhibition, contemporary art had largely fallen into two modes: the theoretical or the political, sometimes both, which were often motivated by the search for identity and community.[25] Eleanor Heartney's review for *Art in America* articulated the exhibition's "representation of a refigured but fragmented collectivity" as a new American identity. She was concerned that the Biennial was "noteworthy not so much for the quality of the art it presents as for the way it mirrors certain disturbing trends within and outside the art world."[26] Disturbing for Heartney particularly was an art without agency, reducing political art to a sign(s) of difference alone, be that race, gender, or ethnicity.

The Biennial was also a bold effort to reframe what was "American" in contemporary American art. It acknowledged vastly diverse heritages in America, not to catalog ethnic and racialized identities but to propose an elimination of totalizing cultural indices, particularly relevant to the many iterations of transnational experience. What Heartney claimed in her critique was that the simple recognition or description of cultural fragmentation trivializes the interventionist capabilities of political art. According to this critique, the Biennial lacked art that offered an alternative to the oppression it addressed. Still, the Biennial solidified "signs of difference" as the art world's hot commodity while drawing attention to the need for an art that could jolt viewers beyond either victimhood or complacency. Meanwhile, speculation and debate around more inclusive curation made a favorable climate for the exhibition of Neshat's work.

Homi Bhabha's contribution to the 1993 Biennial catalog advanced the postcolonial theorist's writings on art and identity and his advocation of "liminal space." In this essay, Bhabha approached the near future of theoretical sophistication in identificatory artistic practice: the transnational artist in the global art market. The liminal space is articulated by artists whose identity makes them capable of "translation between cultures ...effected through the exacerbation of what is culturally incommensurable or strange, which then allows an understanding of the 'Other' to emerge from an elision, an uncanny alienation, of one's own cultural priority."[27] Neshat intervened into the viewer's space of knowledge by introducing a familiar medium (photography, installation) and a familiar subject (the stereotyped, veiled woman) but imbuing alternative articulation (calligraphy, Persian poetry). This disruption prompts viewers to reconsider the subjectivity portrayed, both with and without familiar cultural references in a liminal space Bhabha further defined as "in between the designations of either end from settling into primordial polarities."

The Whitney Biennial was in part a curatorial response to the recent Quincentennial celebrations of America, and yet was blasted for homogenizing collective identities. Jean-Hubert Martin's *Magiciens de la Terre* at the Pompidou and Rasheed Araeen's *The Other Story* which traveled in England were both seminal exhibitions in 1989 that helped advance an era of curation with greater representation of diverse artists, although the resulting efforts did not always exclude ethnocentric approaches to curation. Neshat's work was also criticized as a placation to neo-Orientalist exoticism, not to mention passing curatorial trends. Criticism drawn from the Iranian diaspora were, in Neshat's view, based on a strident opposition to the interruption of Iranian culture by Islamists such that "they cannot even tolerate any dialogue" about the issues the photographs broached.[28] Many viewers found her images too direct, and therefore overly outspoken, or *siasyeh* (she is political).[29] Conversely, addressing martyrdom and jihad with a generalized audience in Europe or America was unavoidably controversial for their associations with terrorism.

Traveling back and forth between Iran and the US, Neshat physically and intellectually embodies the liminal space Bhabha contiguously addressed. She had only ever experienced living in predominantly Westernized societies, whether under Pahlavi or in the US, and now witnessing a homeland where even one's physical appearance was policed was more difficult to comprehend. Neshat's undertaking, what she has referred to as her obsession with understanding, fulfilled her need to resolve these extreme polarities, and thereby her own dual identity. Following the Franklin Furnace exhibition, Neshat abandoned installation to experiment further with the photographic portrait. Enlarging the scale of the prints and adding more militant subjects, *Women of Allah* was first shown at Anina Nosei Gallery in New York in 1995. Later that year, several images from the series were given a room at the 46th Venice Biennale. In 1997, a second commercial gallery, Marco Noire Contemporary Arts, published her first catalog, *Women of Allah*, to accompany a solo exhibition in Turin. Art Speak Gallery in Vancouver published an additional catalog that year. The dissemination of her work through these catalogs was central to her rising career, as was *Shirin Neshat: Women of Allah*, a 1998 solo exhibition at the European House of Photography in Paris. Within just five years of her first exhibition at a small space in Lower Manhattan, Neshat had become a prominent international artist.

Exoticism as Strategy

A surge in scholarship among Euro-American art historians, particularly after 1980, investigated the genre of Orientalism as a mode of visual representation by which power of the "West" over the "East" mirrored colonialist expansion and its ideologies. Scholars such as Linda Nochlin, Donald Rosenthal, and Mary Anne Stevens contributed seminal revisionist investigations of nineteenth-century artists such as Jean-León Gérôme, who painted hyper-realistic images to suggest a transparent window onto an "authentic" Oriental world of harems, belly-dancers, and bathhouses, in which all women lie languidly unclothed. The Orientalist fantasy offered beautiful women in apparent sexual availability to the European male gaze for which they were primarily intended. In many of Gérôme's works, for example, at least one subject is turned away from the viewer for easy viewing of an ample derrière, conventionally relegating the female as object to the time-worn tradition of Western art since the sixteenth-century, if not providing an example of what Clement Greenburg later aligned with kitsch.

The theory that such representations were offered as source knowledge justifying Imperialist conquest was influentially positioned by Edward Said.

But even his pivotal work, *Orientalism* (1978), did not strongly address the role of gender in this paradigm. In *Rethinking Global Sisterhood: Western Feminism & Iran,* Nima Naghibi asserts that Western representations of Muslim women in both art and literature had remained basically unchanged since the late nineteenth-century. Photo postcards from colonized countries like Algiers, popular between 1900 and 1930, also evoked an image of the seductive, sequestered woman for Western consumers. Like the paintings of Gérôme – or of Jean-August-Dominque Ingres, Eugène Delacroix, Henri Matisse, etc. – the postcard, an art of multiples collectible for travelers to foreign lands, satisfied and disseminated a male fantasy of sexually available women in these colonized territories. As photographs, they offered a greater sense of veracity of veiled women as exotic, sexual, passive, and easily conquered, attaching visual metaphor to a primitive Orient.

The transgressive force of Neshat's photographs was scaffolded upon similar ahistorical uses of exoticized subjects in visual culture. The image of the veiled woman is suspended in time within a transparent continuity that racializes and nationalizes the subject in the name of conquest, whether militaristic or economic. The Iranian female body is the rupture in modernity that is sutured according to the needs of both nation-state and Imperialist authority. Meanwhile images of Muslim women satisfied a voyeuristic, European gaze, shielding and preserving the middle-class mythology of its own women as virtuous and chaste. Into the twentieth-century and among nations globally, a woman's standard role was within the home and expectations of her decorum were paramount to the socio-political structure. In Iran, a woman's *sharm* (modesty) was represented by her manner of dress and careful concealment of her body. By 1936, when Reza Shah passed the Unveiling Act, women were forced to discard that belief and from then their bodies were veiled and unveiled accordingly to the nationalistic program at stake.

The static image of the veiled woman, whether found in the press or the painting, the photograph or the vintage postcard, affords the viewer casual contemplation. To direct the gaze, as in Neshat's portraits, is a negation of gender limitations, whether decorum in the West or sharm in the East. The colonialist fantasies of an exotic/erotic Oriental woman entered multiculturalism to be reengaged by "cultural studies that helped to further the understanding of Third World peoples' relations to modernity, the production of images, and the question of self-identity."[30] Performativity in portraiture is a complex extension of the body, producing a unique subjectivity whether stemming from culture or nature. The legacy of artist-as-subject has precedence as a form of resistance to modernist art and its hierarchies, and feminist artists understood the body's ability to inflect meaning. As Amelia Jones observes: "Body artists *perform* rather than *suppress*" making the viewer aware "of the impossibility of determining meaning or identity in any final way and of the contingency of the subject (here the artist as well as the interpreter)."[31] In the 1970s and 1980s, feminist artists and artists of color used appropriation as a crucial strategy to expose visual systems that marginalized gender and race. The purposes of Neshat's images in relation to Iran, Islam, or the US may be ambiguous politically, but their performative aspects referenced such appropriative strategies. Performativity was central to Jones's investigation of the photos of Hannah Wilke who, like Neshat, was called into question regarding the motivations underlying her work. In the 1970s, Wilke's self-portraiture was labeled narcissistic and placating to male desire. More correctly, her complexly appropriated iterations of sexual and gendered norms using her own nude, conventionally beautiful body, collapsed distinctions between the desiring subject and the object desired. Cindy Sherman also enacted and performed gendered stereotypes in her *Film Stills* series of photographs from the same period, and artists used portraiture to disavow rather than establish stable subject representations, including Catherine Opie, Yasumasa Morimura, and Renee Cox. This path toward the social and psychological disruption of preconceived stereotypes via the artist's own body has been paved since the 1960s, when Carolee Schneemann famously stated "I could be an image, but not an Image-maker creating my own self-image" in reference to *36 Transformative Actions*, a series of photographs she had taken of herself in her studio-loft.[32] Schneemann's "transformative actions," their self-performative nature captured in the photograph, placed her in control of her own representation, thus emphasizing her position as the creative artist and object of the performance/gaze simultaneously.

What each of these artists ultimately share with Neshat is that they shifted the concept of what a portrait, and thereby a subject, can be; a politics of identity often unsettling for viewers, even other artists. As with the accusations of erotic narcissism positioned by feminist artists against Wilke, Neshat's detractors included other Iranian artists who viewed her photos as a self-exoticization.[33] Rather than deny Wilke's "narcissism," Jones appropriated it to explain the artist's performative strategy, offering that Wilke's transgression of the boundaries of acceptable identity politics served to raise potent questions about social and cultural structures of female sexuality. Neshat's backlash is also similar to that of Yoko Ono, accused of intentionally negotiating her Asian body in live performance to solidify her status within white, avant-garde circles that embraced a fashionable interest in Zen philosophy during the 1960s.[34] In the case of either Ono or Neshat, whether or not they intended to use their perceived "exotic" subjectivity in works for Euro-American audiences, criticism of their motivations reveal the disparities between white/ Western and non-white/non-Western artists engaged in performance. Using Jones's reassessment of Wilke's "narcissism" and the artists' shared genealogy of performative portraiture, Neshat's project is similarly aligned with a strategic interrogation of the mechanisms upon which exoticisms operate.

This question of exoticism is then predicated upon an inside/outside discourse of the transnational or diasporic artist curated within Western

exhibitions. Hamid Keshmirshekan places "exoticism" within Western viewer's expectations, rather than artist intent. This position is fortified by Gerardo
Mosquera, who asserts that exoticism rests elsewhere in the West's demand
for "authenticity," or what I summarize as a totalizing cultural representation,
which should be replaced by an emphasis upon "strategies of recontextualiza-
tion, appropriation, and recycling."[35] These strategies require both the production and reworking of representations, as well as cultural codes that produce
exoticism. Detectable within Neshat's photographic series, these strategies
are also addressed in the writings of Coco Fusco, who has cited that the deeply
ingrained expectations for authenticity or cultural representation from non-
white or non-Western artists is rooted in the nineteenth-century ethnographic
displays of non-white people for Euro-American audiences.[36] Jean Fisher also
claimed that the complex facets of Western exhibition's commercial and aesthetic value system have brought curatorial practice to its emphasis on signifiers of cultural difference as the new ethnographic display, or "geo-ethnic
entertainment." Further for Fisher, it is not the artist that exoticizes herself,
but the dominance of the Euro-American curatorial framework that "evaluates all cultural productions through its own criteria of otherness [and] ignores
their individual insights."[37] She goes on to point out that such evaluations are
rarely prescribed to white Western artists.

Although Keshmirshekan was speaking of a community of artists exhibiting globally and working from within Iran, his impressions were also
informed by the global art complex and its curatorial interest in the Middle
East. Keshmirshekan, as well as Iftikhar Dadi, observed that such curation
accelerated after 9/11. Dadi complicated exoticism when he described *Women
of Allah* as allegorical images. Basing his interpretation on the subjects' perceived lack of setting or affect – in personality or emotion – he framed them
as depthless signifiers absent of narrative substance, thereby readily reduced
to signs of otherness for Western viewers. However, Neshat's tightly enclosed
portraits of expressionless sitters resist the veil's multiple and potent symbols.
The deployment of direct stares is subversive to Iran's mandatory dress code
that additionally appeals to the Muslim woman's downcast gaze. But for Dadi,
titles such as *I Am Its Secret* evoke allegorical reading, and the presence of
calligraphy is more important as a sign than its interpretation as a text. He
asserts that the images, which he compares to practices of portraiture, pho-
tojournalism, and documentation vis-à-vis Conceptual Art, and the writing,
which he assesses as technically and aesthetically short of the standards of
calligraphic mastery, eschew aesthetic quality for the substantiation of the
allegorical sign.[38] Whereas in the Western tradition allegories retain specific
meanings, Dadi's understanding of contemporary allegory rests upon the
ambiguity of Neshat's photos that serve to further distance the viewer from
the subject. This reading of the subjects as "transcultural allegories" suggests
that the artist offers the Muslim woman as the ambivalent yet resistant sign of
a flattened Other for Western spectatorial consumption.

I wrestle with Dadi's allegorical turn in so far as it dismisses the images' performativity, and I do not agree that Neshat dispensed with aesthetic quality to emphasize affect. Calligraphy appears exotic in part due to its abstraction, incomprehensible to those who are also incapable of assessing its quality. Further, if the aesthetics of the script were a factor, Neshat could have gained access to more masterful calligraphers to execute the writing, further insisting writing as a performative act. Igor Zabel described his initial perception of the photos as a "gap" between their pleasing formal qualities and the apparent content, "a mixture of old and more recent stereotypes…. about the 'Orient,' the Middle East, and the Muslim world" and Hamid Dabashi described a similar gap in his viewing, between "seduction and sadness, violence and serenity."[39] The inherent dichotomies on display in the subjects, like violence and beauty, contrast sharply with the artificial odalisques, interrupting the opacity of Orientalist fantasy that harem images perpetuate. According to this visual logic, identity can be produced and/or destabilized through the body, and Neshat embodies/performs the veiled woman as Muslim Other because, as Zabel assessed, attempting to correct that image would only fail. Instead, she "simulates it, making us aware of its constructed, artificial nature," which is perhaps more productive than offering alternative images. For Dabashi, in performing the veil, she "stages the culturally constituted body in an overwhelmingly exaggerated way" that, I believe, forces the viewer to consider the depths of the subject rather than her surface. Directing the viewer's gaze away from superficial representation and into the experiential domain of embodiment, Neshat's interplay, between recognizing a role and performing it, and the viewer's co-recognition of the performative act, recall what Jones referred to as "the pose," in which performers consciously enact an established identity without clarifying their position on that identity. By extension, realization of the powerlessness of the female body to control its own meaning, independent of its interpretation as cultural sign, resonates with special acuity for viewers whose bodies are similarly demarcated.

Allegory and stereotype are both steeped in repetition, and the seriality of Neshat's self-consciously performed images reveal and deflate the potency of their neo-Orientalist associations, informed as they are by strategies and practices of appropriation and by feminist artists who preceded her. From this latter influence is the act of "posing" as also understood by Craig Owens. Differing slightly from Jones's concept, but aligning with Schneemann's now-famous statement, Owens said that with portraiture in contemporary art practice, "The subject poses as an object in order to become a subject."[40] One can also apply here Judith Butler's concept of "parody" and the power of imitation; it is through parody that one reveals the culturally constructed nature of identity. Neshat's only lived experience in chador would have been during her visits to Iran, and therefore her pose for camera is crucial to her intent. Within her portraiture is an embodied exercise by which Neshat utilized an ostensibly feminist art practice in a radical reevaluation of the Orientalized subject. But to read Neshat's photos as contingent to feminist or contemporary art is not to narrowly affix them to comparative Western art movements. Rather, this underscores a transnational, transcultural practice emboldened by the visual tools and strategies at her disposal. A strength of Neshat's early photographs is that they fused many approaches that complicate any singular understanding or clear articulation of socio-political position. They only emphasize Neshat's own fragmentation, having lived in the US for twenty years by this period.

Between the viewer's space and the pictorial space of the image, the process of disruption and estrangement strips spectatorship of complacency when the subject has control of its own depiction. Neshat's discomforting gaze guides the viewer to an awareness of the act of looking, foregrounded by colonial legacies and sexual politics. Perhaps the most powerful tool in this arsenal for control over meaning is the refusal of visual pleasure, specifically long assumed to belong to the male spectator and by which women are the "bearers rather than the makers of meaning," the objects of a "scopophilic, fetishizing, and inexorably male desire."[41] The body as a site of meaning, defined by patriarchal codes like colonialism and politics, is reclaimed by Neshat as a site of intervention. According to Janet Wolff, who framed a "cultural politics of the body," it is this awareness of the body's status as culturally produced that leads to "self-surveillance."[42] This establishes patriarchy as a reciprocal exchange, under which self-surveilling creates a discursive construct for the feminine ideal. In performing the image of the devoted Muslim woman in Iran, Neshat engages in a staged surveillance of herself, collaborating with the presumed knowledge of Western viewers while denying them the pleasure of wholly possessing that knowledge. The viewer is held at bay, obscured by a screen of calligraphy that both maintains and subverts the Muslim female identity before them.

Neshat's photographs were far more invested in complicating established stereotypes of the Muslim woman than offering alternatives, revealing instead the impossibility of fixed identity. This complexity of identity may best be captured by an untitled work from *Women of Allah*. The text is taken again from Farrokhzad's *I Feel Sorry for the Garden*. A close frame of Neshat's face, her hand held up to slightly parted lips, draws attention to a part of the body associated with communication and language as well as sexuality and desire. For the exhibition *Without Boundary: Seventeen Ways of Looking*, Fereshteh Daftari also described the gesture as the "signal of a kiss" or "self-imposed silence," but the reference to the hamsa or Saqqakhaneh adds more layers of meaning. Sussan Babaie compared Farrokhzad's verse on the fingers against the circular field on the hand that contains a Shi'a incantation for Abbas, another martyred hero of Karbala.[43] The contradictions between socio-religious pride and here Farrokhzad's lament for women's rights further situate the complexities for women who, although loyal to the nation, are overwhelmed by its ideologies. The circular writing on the back of the hand recalls decorative mosque medallions while the intimacy and sexuality of the gesture, transgressive to an Islamist, would titillate the Orientalist. And yet either spectator is held at distance by the hand before the lips and its simultaneous gesture of silence, implicating the female self-surveillance imposed under both Islamist and Imperialist patriarchy.

From the scopophilic object of fetishistic desire to the abject object of alterity, Neshat's subjects emerge from and against historical and mainstream representations that would silence them. They suggest agency and control over their own meaning because, according to Stuart Hall, the position from which one speaks or writes is an enunciation.[44] Neshat's enunciation is from three positions: the US, from where she watched her country's revolution; Iran, which she had once known intimately and was now concerned to relearn; and the spatio-temporal impact of past and present that coalesce in a transnational identity. Both Jones and Owens established an understanding of self-imaging in photography with debt to Roland Barthes:

> The photograph (the one I intend) represents the very subtle moment when... I am neither subject nor object but a subject who feels he is becoming an object: I then experience a micro-version of death: I am truly becoming a specter.[45]

Self-portraits are by nature performative due to the sitter's role in the construction of self as subject-object. In her self-portraits, Neshat as both subject and object addresses the photographs of Muslim identity circulating in the media; only by participating in the inauthenticity of these representations can she subvert their power through performance. The exaggeration implicit to performance and still-photographic representations conspires with the viewer's foregrounded knowledge within a new dialectical space that exposes the artifice of representation itself. The relationship between Neshat's images as performative portraits invites reevaluation of presumed knowledge, and thereby the viewer's own subject position. This "interpretive exchange," to use Jones's phrase, takes place discursively between artist, viewer, and culture at large to question meanings that performance exaggerates. Self-conscious performances of identity privilege "ironicized modes of photographic display" in the contemporary period and imbricate the relationship between documentary and fiction. Neshat's photographic deployments, like her video installations and films to follow, service the technological apparatus toward "forgetting the world in order to remember it [and] produce images caught between referentiality and representation."[46] *Unveiling* and *Women of Allah* repurposed static images of Iranian women as powerfully complex subjects recognized in and through an embodied space, suspending viewers and the subjects in reflexively interpretive exchanges. Resisting imposed narratives through their inherent silence, they remind us that bodies can be both inscribed by and sources of meaning, capable of stripping the layers that allow new histories to emerge.

Notes

1 Miranda, Carolina A. "Artist Shirin Neshat challenges the idea of Muslim women as victims and explores exile." *Los Angeles Times* (October 23, 2019).
2 MacDonald, Scott. "Between Two Worlds: An Interview with Shirin Neshat." *Feminist Studies*, vol. 30, no. 3. (Fall, 2004). p. 625. Here, Neshat also discusses the collaboration with her photographers.
3 Ibid., 627.
4 Ibid.
5 Sadeghi, Andrea. "Twenty-Nine Degrees." *The Daily California*, vol. XIII, no. 174. (Aug 6–12, 1982). p. 8.
6 Neshat, Shirin. MFA Thesis Exhibition Statement (Aug., 1982). University of Berkeley Art Museum & Pacific Film Archive.
7 MacDonald, Scott. "Between Two Worlds: An Interview with Shirin Neshat," p. 627.
8 Ibid.
9 Camhi, Leslie. "Lifting the Veil." *ARTNews*, vol. 99, no. 2 (Feb., 2000), 149–151. p. 150.
10 Birbragher, Francine. "Shirin Neshat: Interview." *Art Nexus*, vol. 2, no. 50 (Sept.–Nov., 2003). p. 92.
11 Ibid.
12 Zaya, Octavio. "Q&A Shirin Neshat: Islamic Women as Ambiguous Icons." p. 18.
13 Marks, Laura U. *The Skin of the Film: Intercultural Cinema, Embodiment, and the Senses.* Durham, NC: Duke University Press, 2000, p. 88.
14 Neshat's Exhibition Proposal to Franklin Furnace, 1992. Franklin Furnace Archives, Brooklyn, NY.
15 Malik, Amna. "Surface Tension: Reconsidering Horizontality in the Work of Diasporic Iranian Artists." Harris, Jonathan ed. *Identity Theft: The Cultural Colonization of Contemporary Art.* Liverpool: Liverpool University Press, 2008. 109–134. p. 110.
16 Balaghi, Shiva & Lynn Gumpert. *Picturing Iran: Art, Society, & Revolution.* New York: I.B. Tauris & Co., 2002. Passim. Balaghi builds upon Islamic scholar Annemarie Schimmel's understanding of the roots of calligraphy and textual meaning to offer her interpretation of Parviz Tanavoli's adoption of abstract form.
17 Malik, Amna. "Dialogues Between 'Orientalism' & Modernism in Shirin Neshat's Women of Allah" in Jeffrey & Minissale's *Global & Local Art Histories.* Newcastle: Cambridge Scholars Publishing, 2007. p. 165.
18 Larson, Jacqueline. "What if the Object Should Shoot?: Shirin Neshat's 'Women of Allah' as Veiled Criticism." *Shirin Neshat's Women of Allah.* Vancouver: Art Speak Gallery, 1997. p. 12. Larson discusses the alternate translations. However, in a collection of poems by Farrokhzad translated by Ahmad Karimi-Hakkak, the author also suggests this line in the narrator's voice as "its mind emptying of green memories." See *Remembering the Flight: Twenty Poems by Forrough Farrokhzad.* Port Coquitlin, BC: Nik Publishers, 1997.
19 Scheiwiller, Staci Gem. "In the House of Fatemeh: Revisiting Shirin Neshat's Photographic Series Women of Allah." Scheiwiller eds. *Performing the Iranian State:*

Visual Culture and Representations of Iranian Identity. (201–220). London: Anthem Press, 2013, p. 204.

20 Jones, Ann Rosalind. "Writing the Body: Toward an Understanding of l'Ecriture Feminine." *Feminist Studies*, vol. 7, no. 2 (Summer 1981). p. 252.

21 Zaya, Octavio. "Q&A Shirin Neshat: Islamic Women as Ambiguous Icons." *Creative Camera* (Oct./Nov. 1996). p. 18.

22 Khazini, Dorna. "Shirin Neshat." *The Believer* (Aug., 2003). 95–105. p. 97.

23 Birbragher, Francine. "Shirin Neshat: Interview," p. 91

24 Heartney, Eleanor. "Shirin Neshat: Living Between Cultures." *After the Revolution: Women Who Transformed Contemporary Art.* New York: Prestel, 2007. p. 233.

25 Foster, Hal; Rosalind Krauss; Silvia Klolbowski; Miwon Kwon; Benjamin Buchloh. "The Politics of the Signifier: A Conversation on the Whitney Biennial." *October,* vol. 66 (Autumn, 1993). 3–27. p. 3.

26 Heartney, Eleanor. "Identity Politics at the Whitney." *Art in America* (May, 1993). 43–47, p. 47.

27 Bhabha, Homi. "Beyond the Pale: Art in the Age of Multicultural Translation." 1993 Whitney Biennial Catalog. New York: The Whitney Museum of American Art & Harry N. Abrams, 1993. 62–73. p. 64.

28 Birbragher, Francine. "Shirin Neshat: Interview," p. 9o.

29 Zanganeh, Lila Azam eds. *My Sister, Guard Your Veil; My Brother, Guard Your Eyes: Uncensored Iranian Voices.* Boston: Beacon Press, 2006. p. 44–54.

30 Grewal, Inderpal. *Transnational America: Feminisms, Diasporas, Neoliberalisms.* Durham: Duke University Press, 2005. p. 211.

31 Jones, Amelia. *Body Art: Performing the Subject.* Minneapolis: University Minnesota Press, 1998. p. 58.

32 Jones, Amelia. "Postfeminism, Feminist Pleasures, & Embodied Theories of Art" Frueh, Langer, & Raven eds. *New Feminist Criticism.* New York: Icon Editions, 1994. p. 30.

33 Honigman, Ana Fidel. "Against the Exotic." *ArtReview* (Sept. 2005), p. 97. Also see Khaleeli, Homa. "Salome: straight outta Tehran." *The Guardian* (Jan. 4, 2011).

34 Rhee, Jieun. "Performing the Other: Yoko Ono's Cut Piece." *Art History,* vol. 28, pt. 1, (Feb. 2005). 96–115. p. 98. Rhee's thesis is primarily based on *Cut Piece*, performed in New York in 1965. However, Ono was sought by Fluxus founder George Maciunas, and her reluctance to join an organized art movement has been documented. Her own relationship to Zen Buddhism and her incorporation of its premises into her work was evident for more than a decade before *Cut Piece.*

35 Keshmirshekan, Hamid. "The Question of Identity vis-à-vis Exoticism in Contemporary Iranian Art." *Iranian Studies,* vol. 43, no. 4 (Sept. 2010). p. 500.

36 Fusco, Coco. "The Other History of Intercultural Performance." *TDR,* vol. 38, no. 1 (Spring, 1994). p. 145.

37 Fisher, Jean. "The Syncretic Turn: Cross-Cultural Practices in the Age of Multiculturalism," in *Theory in Contemporary Art Since 1985,* Zoya Kocur and Simon Leung eds. (Oxford 2005); quoted in Hamid Kesmirshekan, "The Question of Identity vis-à-vis Exoticism in Contemporary Iranian Art," *Iranian Studies,* 43, no. 4 (Sept. 2010), 501.

38 Dadi, Iftikhar. "Shirin Neshat's Photographs as Postcolonial Allegories." *Signs,* vol. 34, no. 1 (Autumn 2008). p. 137.

39 Zabel, Igor. "Women in Black." *Art Journal* vol. 60, no. 4 (Winter 2001). 16–25. p. 25.

40 Dabashi, Hamid. "Bordercrossings: Shirin Neshat's Body of Evidence." *Shirin Neshat.* Castello di Rivoli Museo de Arte, 2002. p. 37.

41 Owens, Craig. *Beyond Recognition: Representation, Power, and Culture.* Los Angeles: University of California Press, 1992, p. 215.

42 Mulvey, Laura. "Visual Pleasure & Narrative Cinema." Jones, Amelia ed. *The Feminism & Visual Culture Reader*. New York: Routledge, 2003. Originally published in *Screen,* vol. 16, no. 3 (Autumn 1975). p. 6–18.

43 Wolff, Janet. "Reinstating Corporeality: Feminism & Body Politics." Amelia Jones ed. *The Feminism and Visual Culture Reader*. New York: Routledge Press, 2003. p. 416–417.

44 Hall, Stuart. "Cultural Identity & Diaspora." Rutherford, Lawrence, & Wishat eds. *Identity: Community, Culture, & Difference*. London: Lawrence & Wishat, 1990. p. 222.

45 Jones, Amelia. *Self/Image: Technology, Representation, & the Contemporary Subject*. New York: Routledge Press, 2006. p. 39.

46 Balsom, Erika. *Exhibiting Cinema in Contemporary Art*. Amsterdam: Amsterdam University Press, 2013. p. 183.

2 Spectacle of Memory
Embodied Experience in Neshat's Early Video Installations

In 1996, Neshat produced an installation for "Art in the Anchorage," one of Creative Time's many projects that fill abandoned or underutilized public spaces with visual art. Within the cavernous cells beneath the Brooklyn Bridge, known as the Anchorage, Neshat created a self-portrait in motion: an image of her face in close-up, swaddled in black headscarf, projected onto a vertical screen. Untitled, the work has come to be recorded as *Anchorage* (Figure 2.1), a video performance enacting gestures of her still photography and marking a pivotal transition toward video. This chapter turns to the expanding role of the moving-image after 1990 and its significance to globality at the turn of the century. Neshat describes her filmic contributions to this period as "video installation" and fitted an embodied spectatorship to their continued explorations of gender and oppression, diaspora, and memory. As much acclaim as they garnered, these video installations are largely excluded from historiography of the period's "cinematic turn," affixed as they were to ethnocentric discourse.

Video projection of Super-8 film had been an installation element of the work at Franklin Furnace, its nostalgic graininess associated with the home movies of the 1970s in both Iran and the US. But *Anchorage* was a stand-alone video, just four minutes long, a single projection of Neshat's hands and face in total darkness. The sound element of the work is her own improvised chanting, one of three activities included in her performance. In a sequence of edits, her hands begin outstretched, proper to the gesture of submissive prayer, then suddenly hold a revolver aimed at the viewer. Rather than the static image of her photos, Neshat's revolver functions and fires at the viewer. In the final images, she swirls and chants, eyes closed in an incantation of the Sufis' whirling dervish dance.

As a performance-for-camera, engaging in image significations that vacillate between Islamist terror and Islamic spirituality, *Anchorage* enacted representations that both rely upon and counteract exoticisms. In its order of movements, the Muslim woman is manifest by reference to religious culture, then to the violence associated with that culture, and lastly with spiritual liberation. The dervish dance is reduced to a sign of otherness within the context

DOI: 10.4324/9781003341192-3

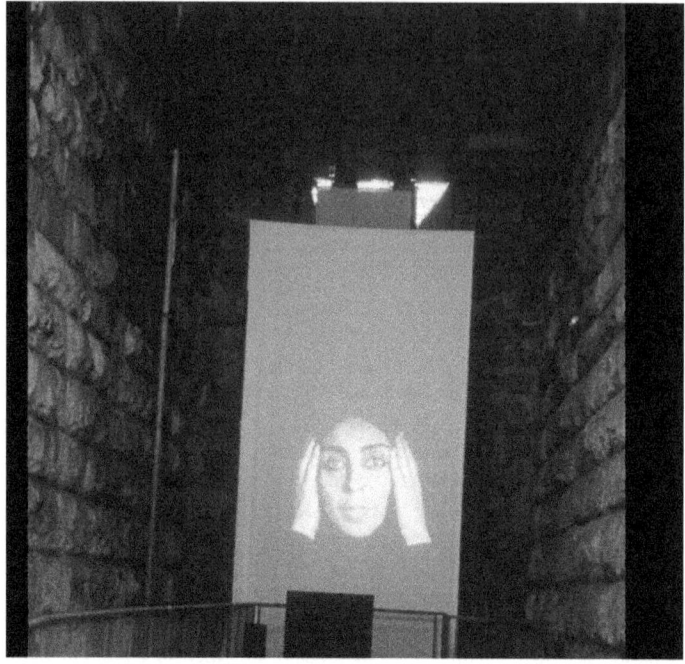

Figure 2.1 Anchorage, 1996. Video (installation view). Courtesy Creative Time Archive, Fales Library and Special Collections, New York University Libraries, © Shirin Neshat.

of Western viewership; the indecipherable text of the photos is replaced by unfamiliar music and movement. Like the Persian poems written across the body, the veiled body's enactment of song and dance are the cultural elements that embed the work with notions of "Islam," an exoticism intended to seduce the viewer who is lured into an exchange of stereotypes accommodating the colonial West, only to be confronted by her gun and her gaze.

These effects retain qualities of early experiments in performance-for-camera, particularly by women. Lynda Benglis's *On Screen* (1972), for example, presents a subject sans narrative, in which the artist taped a series of uncomfortable facial expressions directed toward the viewer and in front of a television monitor of subsequent images of herself in these same contorted expressions. Benglis's interaction arguably fulfills an identity reliant upon the screen itself, and the viewer is a witness to the inauthenticity of mediated representation. Neshat similarly implicated herself as the object for viewing with a close-up portrait and a black background, simultaneously disarming and unsettling viewers through her direct gaze and profound gestures. The connection Neshat extended to the viewer through the frontality of her projected image is rooted in the previous photographs, but the cinematic quality of a subject enacted in the darkened space below the Brooklyn Bridge intensified the viewing experience. Amelia Jones's explanation of a heightened relationship between the artist/self and audience/other is an intense viewership she posits as "intersubjectivity:" the self-realization of the viewer that occurs through the spectatorship of an artist's self-actualization on screen.[1] Via intersubjectivity, Jones supports an understanding of early single-channel videos, such as Benglis's *On Screen*, in which use of the body emphasize the subject as the object of viewing. In other words, by acknowledging the subjectivity of the projected body on the screen the viewer must, in turn, acknowledge their own. This is the result of an inherent intimacy with that which is on screen or monitor, created under certain viewing conditions such as projection in a dramatic, darkened space.

The intersubjectivity between bodies-viewing and bodies-viewed occurring, as it does for Jones, through and against the distanciating effects of performance, underpins Neshat's forthcoming video work. For instance, one could consider *Anchorage* a video-portrait, imbued with the same psychological suspension of the subject as her photo-portraits, the same contradictory impulses of seduction and repulsion. To this end, Laura Mulvey's 'possessive spectator,' building from Raymond Bellour's 'pensive spectator,' is one who, confronted with an autonomous film subject, unconsciously desires mastery over that subject.[2] If Neshat's photos created a sense of anxiety, a loss of command over the subject, her videos extended that anxiety into a filmic complexity and ambiguity by which subjects on view, unhinged from the confines of strict narration, offer another kind of intersubjectivity that Maria Walsh calls 'entrancement,' also prefixed by Bellour's insistence upon the hypnotic experience of 'cinema-situation.' Occurring in moments at which narrative guidance is replaced by an "intense proximity to an image quality,"[3] these affectations were typical to an influx of moving-image works in the 1990s, employing sound, space, and high-quality cinematography toward a phenomenology of spectacle on par with entrancement. No less will be noted of Neshat's approach to video installation in which her consideration of site and architecture, both within the film and that of the viewing space, aligned with an intentionality toward place-making and the fusion of visual art and cinema. To understand the theoretical framework undergirding the convergence of art and cinema in this era, Erika Balsom's insightful connections between film media and contemporary art exhibition and Laura Marks's theories of intercultural film are pivotal.

With Balsom, the growing trend of cinematic experience within exhibitions is important for understanding the appeal of Neshat's work to curators. She pinpoints its beginning to about 1990, an era in which "cinema enters the gallery on the tide of a culture converging under the sign of the digital" during which millimeter film, to which Neshat will also turn, is easily digitized and disseminated, aligned with mass culture accessibility of the movie theater and the avant-garde usage of a nostalgic media.[4] After *Anchorage,* Neshat recognized photography's limited capacity to communicate philosophical ideas beyond political messages, and perhaps realized the immediacy of video to elicit an intersubjectivity, or embodied experience, with the audience.[5] Marks notes the phenomena of film's "temporal immediacy" between viewer and object, "more like being in physical contact than facing a representation."[6] Neshat described her still images as reminiscent of the West's fascination with the Muslim subject, but today there encapsulate the additional "political implications that have altered our fairy-tale image about the Middle East, because the Oriental is now a terrorist."[7] As these images begin to move, she remained committed to interrogating the cultural climate of Iran but sought to communicate an understanding of Iranian subjectivity from her viewpoint: the personal ramifications of oppression resulting in exile. In the next chapter, controversies of that viewpoint will be addressed alongside the promise and problems of global contemporary art at the century's turn. Here, I will attempt to recontextualize Neshat's early video installations within the historical framework of the 'cinematic turn' in art, particularly as an immersive practice sited within museum and international exhibition.

Although rooted in the literary works of Toni Morrison, I also situate Neshat's videos as a practice of 'rememory.' This is in part possible through film's transitory ability to crystallize specters of history. Marking intercultural film to 1985, Marks arrests film's ability to evoke memory through embodied knowledge, in the viewer's response to a sensory experience of place emergent through an affectation of image quality she calls "haptic visuality." Neshat's video installations are a rememory of a lost past, traversing through and against diasporic nostalgia to confront the limits of knowledge and history. Although I will not fully engage haptic visuality, there are many connections that Neshat's affective imagery shares with a corporeal consciousness bridging cinema's appeals to the body. Her sensory video installations further reflect Balsom's insistence that "cinema-themed exhibitions and projected-image installations of high-gloss and bombast underline cinema's novelty in an art institutional context."[8]

High-gloss and bombast aside, Balsom still asserts the transgressive potential of video installation not only in its spectacle novelty, that image-aura which Walsh and Marks fluently define, but in the innovative spaces opened by the hybrid practices of art and cinema. Neshat capitalized on the decade-moment when projection would replace the monitor and, with the spatialization of moving-images made possible in the gallery and museum, new narrative temporalities position a dynamic relationship between past/present, subject/viewer, and home/host. It is against this backdrop that Neshat resisted the limitations of an "ethnic" artist to enter what Hamid Naficy defines as a "transnational genre" of film that provides interventional sites for "intertextual, cross-cultural, and translational struggles over meanings and identities."[9]

Exile in the Shadow of Memory

With film, Neshat's new subjects in motion traverse metaphoric and psychological borders. *The Shadow Under the Web* (1997) (Figure 2.2) was her first filmic exploration of this idea, a further transition from challenging static representation to communicating an embodied experience through screen. The 'shadow' of the five-minute video, spread across four rectangular monitors, is Neshat herself, running between four spaces: a mosque, a crowded *souq* (market), along the ancient city wall, and on the modern streets. The video was locationally filmed in Istanbul for its 1997 Biennial, a city symbolic for centuries as a border between "East and West," a complex space housing large Christian, Muslim, and Jewish populations. However, Neshat's interest in veiled female figures traversing the confines of physical and psychological space was evident as far back as her 1982 MFA thesis:

> My new works are atmospheric environments created to evoke a certain sense of beauty and mystery. My focus has been an imaginary personal approach to the inter-relationship of human beings and their environment.[10]

In chador, Neshat moves through an urbanscape of enclosed spaces including a claustrophobic and imposing series of walls surrounding Istanbul, begun as early as its founding as Constantinople in the fourth-century. But Neshat also passes a vast, industrial wasteland. As with cities in Iran, Istanbul is at once ancient and modern and Neshat, in what seems to be desperation and confusion, navigates herself between these temporal and cultural spaces as the work's central subject. As viewers follow Neshat's trajectory across the four monitors, each installed above eye-level on four walls, the images montage at varying intervals and the viewer's focus is just as divided and overwhelmed as the subject frantically navigating her territory. The experience thereby transmits a bodily anxiety and confusion of a city conquered at various times by Greek, Roman, and Ottoman civilizations.

The Shadow Under the Web resists reduction to a simplistic consideration of Muslim identity. In a major shift, Neshat utilized cinematic space toward a metaphoric position of the Muslim woman within the contemporary world more broadly. That use of urban space recalls the work of Valie Export, who in the 1970s incorporated her body into photographic tableaus interrogating the position of women's presence in environments dominated by man-made design and architecture. In *The Shadow Under the Web,* Neshat highlights a negotiation of spaces between past and present, tradition and progress, and the cross of cultures described as "Eastern" or "Western." Imagery of Neshat running through the streets of Istanbul in chador creates an interstitial moment for the viewer who must also consider their own identity and its relation to physical spaces.

Neshat has described the four backdrops to *The Shadow Under the Web* as private, public, sacred, and natural.[11] This categorization of Istanbul's

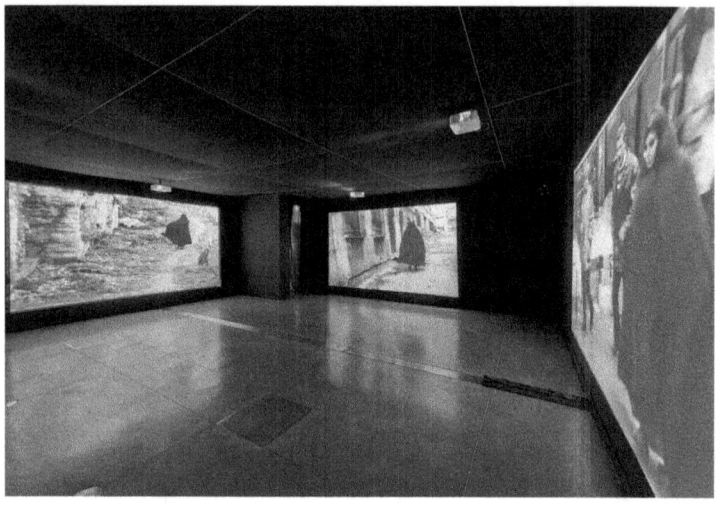

Figure 2.2 The Shadow Under the Web, 1997. Four-channel color video, 10mins. Collection IAC, Villeurbanne/Rhône-Alpes, France. Installation view: *La pratique est absolument necessaire et elle pose désormais le prroblème non plus de son esthétique mais de sa strategie!* Photo by Blaise Adilon. © Shirin Neshat. Originally shown on four rectangular monitors, more recent iterations of the piece are projected.

available vistas is doubtlessly the premise for the work's four-monitor format. The "shadow" inferred by the presence of the running woman represents the lost presences of millions of people who once lived within the walls of Constantinople/Istanbul, the many transferences of power and immigration into the city over the centuries. The pre-recorded sound of Neshat's breath is amplified in the gallery space with an intense echo that elicits the breathlessness of the hurried protagonist. In Nathalie Leleu's description, "The rhythm of her walk gives scansion to the full allegorical measure of Muslim women's exclusion from the public sphere" and curator Francesco Bonami described the implied gendered meaning of the work: men determine cities and their governance while women are forced to exist according to the systems and rules of that governance.[12]

Following *The Shadow Under the Web*, an expression of private space as "feminine" and public space as "masculine" is a consistent theme of Neshat's work, although the gendering of space is not unique to Islam. To Neshat's framing of public space as masculine, or for that matter Valie Export's illumination of the gendered power constructs of architecture, one could add that even the pre-Islamic walls of Istanbul are indicative of the symbolic space of male-determined histories. For Bonami, it was unimportant whether Neshat runs along the inside or outside of the wall, but that her chador-clad presence against it underscores the placement of Muslim women in structured society as "othered" under both Islamic and Christian patriarchies, and these simultaneous transgressions regarding women in society will also characterize her later work.[13]

At the end of her path along the wall is a mosque, but she is unable to enter beyond its iron gates. History and religion are positioned as co-conspirators, from one monitor to the next, in the reduction of its female subject to a metaphoric shadow. Few women in Istanbul wear chador, but the implication is that throughout history women have worn the standards and followed the laws of patriarchal societies, though largely excluded from determining their political or historical fates. In the last of the four projections, the alleys entangle in a web of complicated history, the power of religion, and the consumer realm of the market within which global civilizations converge. In the maze of alleys that represent the city's edges, one may escape an identity limited by historical, religious, cultural, and gendered definitions, and invent new possibilities, if only temporarily.

The Shadow Under the Web marked Neshat's own increased visibility as an internationally exhibiting artist, a migratory status itself based on travel from place to place in the making and exhibition of work, through which space and culture are revealed as fluid, as metaphoric as tangible. One of the first exilic artists to profoundly relate space and identity, Ana Mendieta's *Siluetas* series emphasized possibilities for reclamation or transcendence through an appropriation of the environment. Mendieta carved her body into the land, its mark then photographed and sealed permanently for memory. Recorded as a citizen of the earth, she thereby occupied neither her present in the US nor her past in Cuba. Her phantoms remain as the "specters that leave us looking about anxiously for the person they invoke,"[8] and calls the viewer to face their own transience on earth and the inability of borders to contain them.

Siluetas translates as "shadows," and similarly *The Shadow Under the Web* visualizes a fleeting presence, a specter wrestling against the borders of past and present. Evident in these works is the ability to transgress fixed identities by virtue of a marginalized position. But twentieth-century literature is replete with narratives of exiles in a constant state of lack, and Neshat's own words have been contextualized in a way that reduces her artistic agency: "I've permanently lost a sense of center. I can never call any place home. I will forever be in a state of in-between."[14] This oft-repeated autobiographical statement presents her as an exile obsessively concerned with her homeland, in constant longing for return. It underscored an exotic representative in the West-centric field of 'global' art exhibition and deemphasized the potential of diasporic artists to interculturally translate and transgress meanings via travel and the multiple perspectives it enables. The perspective of the transnational artist exceeds the exilic relationship to fixed locations of home and host countries, based on the physical and psychic conditions produced by travel itself. The effects of globalization on women's lived experiences are asserted in the writings of Inderpal Grewal, Fatima Mernissi, and Caren Kaplan, who have noted how physical travel affects identity. Travel is a suspension in time and space that makes one more aware of her locational positioning and sheds a distanciating light on her place in the world while allowing her to reaffirm and disengage from fixed identity. Naturally, this is easier if the conditions are freely chosen, such as those of the "migrant artist" who is supported by globalization and art's international exhibition.

The installation concept for *The Shadow Under the Web* recalls nascent use of the avant-garde video monitor, such as by Benglis, Joan Jonas, or Dara Birnbaum. But its multi-monitor, experiential model applied recent approaches, such as those by Gary Hill and Bill Viola. Balsom attempts to parallel film's historic media within contemporary art, citing, for example, the nineteenth-century *fin-de-siecle* invention of film with the late twentieth-century artist's hybrid use of the analog (16mm, 35mm) with newly available digital practices. Whether on monitor or screen, "video" as an overarching term to express a visual art engagement with film was, in Chrissie Iles's summation, becoming irrelevant, as artists experimented with various forms both traditional and new (montage, mis-en-scene, multi-projection, illusionism) that overlapped with other media (the body, performance, sculpture).[15] Neshat's evolution from photographer with *Anchorage* (a performative enactment of her photographs) to her future as video artist with *The Shadow Under the Web* (a spatialization of moving images within the gallery space) is an important precursor to her future video installations that coincide the moving-image as visual art. Experimenting with performance-for-camera, color film, single-projection, and monitor, she arrived at black-and-white 16- and 35-mm film, symbolic of the visual landscape of black chadors she witnessed in Iran and evocative of an unspecified ambience of memory.

By an unspecified ambient memory, I mean to align the symbolism of black-and-white film with the past and Neshat's disruption of clear narrative to the service of visual reference. The private history of one's culture, particularly from Neshat's exilic, transnational viewpoint, necessitates resolving, reimagining, and rewriting. Marks suggests "recollection-images" as the intermediary between a lost past and a present at odds with hegemonic narratives. Too painful or too elusive, "a recollection-image embodies a past event that has no match in the present image repertoire."[16] Walsh often categorizes "entrancement" as surrealist style, the melding of recognizable images to indescribable fissures and links between past and present that imply affective imagery above meaningful clarity. Similarly, the "lyrical" and "ambiguous" qualities often ascribed to Neshat's videos still misapprehend their correlations to the exilic experience of history, as "the optical image that cannot be connected to living memory... yet cries out to have a memory assigned to it."[17]

The sensorial immediacy of cinematic form translates the untranslatable textures, signs, and sounds that fill the ineffable gaps between official histories and personal memory. The performance-for-camera of *Anchorage* and the specter of her image on the screens in *The Shadow Under the Web* 'cry out' urgently. Both employ sound rather than speech to create textures of mimesis – the emotive music and gunfire in *Anchorage* and the embodied rhythm of the breath in *Shadow* – and the drama of space to submerge viewers into the subject's present/presence on screen. The darkened, sublime austerity beneath the Brooklyn Bridge attenuated the viewer fully to Neshat's performative gestures, and the dizzying effects of *Shadow's* four monitors on four walls imbricated the viewer's experience with the subject's frantic movements. As a young student, Neshat had solitarily experienced the Revolution of her homeland through the eyes of its principal enemy; her transition to video installation also occurred at a moment of personal upheaval. Her visits to Iran that began in May 1991 abruptly ended in August 1995 when she was detained and interrogated at the Tehran airport. She has not returned to Iran, still ruled by a regime that continues to denounce her work.[18]

Community and Convergence

Briefly introduced in Chapter 1, exhibitions such as the 1993 Whitney Biennial and the Pompidou's *Magiciens de la Terre* contributed to more diverse representations of artists and curatorial themes. Seminal to the understanding of cinema and the moving-image in art, *Passages de L'Image* (1990), curated by Bellour, Catherine David, and Christine van Assche, was also staged by the Pompidou. David would go on to head the 1997 Documenta, and Harald Szeemann's turn at the 1999 Venice Biennale also secured the prominence of the moving-image in contemporary exhibitions. The convergence of interests in globalism and identities, the spectacle experience of the exhibition, and the integration of cinema with art laid the foundation for the "novelty of the new." Balsom asserts that this newness easily emerged within spaces between art and cinema that allowed for new narratives, temporalities, and images.

With film, Neshat intended to confront the fragmented ways in which cultural identities, including the exile herself, are reconstructed within dominant cinematic and visual representations in the West. *Anchorage* and *The Shadow Under the Web* asserted a new position of agency by presenting a previously marginalized subject engaged in empowered actions or struggling to self-actualize against the psychological and social restraints of space. But by employing herself as subject, Neshat emphasized marginalization or isolation as a personal experience of displacement more than a diasporic one. With her transition into the trilogies she began to surround herself with other Iranians: filmmakers, editors, screenwriters, and composers versed in Iranian film history. With the assistance of Shoja Azari and Ghasem Ebrahimian, she progressed from *The Shadow Under the Web* to more complex productions, from color video to 16mm film, from the artist-in-performance to a cast of players. Just as she conceived and designed imagery undertaken by photographers for *Unveiling* and *Women of Allah*, Neshat's new work was the result of intense collaboration. They helped with the execution of concepts she discussed through storyboards, scouted film sites, and edited the postproduction footage. By 1997, these filmic collaborations had become the nexus of her artistic focus. She resigned from The Storefront, and her marriage to Kyong Park ended.

The division of labor apparent in Neshat's collaboration with Iranian filmmakers is not out of the ordinary. After 1990, it was common for artists to leave the avant-garde approaches of video and its single-artist model and enter a cinematic process with an expansive crew of professionally trained filmmakers. Such productions were undertaken by artists fortunate to procure necessary funding, and Neshat's contemporaries Sam Taylor-Johnson and Steve McQueen spring to mind. With growing international success and evidence of her interest in filmmaking, Neshat was picked up by Chelsea-based Gladstone Gallery, who also represented Matthew Barney. Meanwhile, the increased appearance of video installation in exhibitions coincided with the international popularity of Iranian film that took shape in the early 1990s after the death of Ayatollah Khomeini and the loosening of strict supervision of Iran's motion picture industry under the Ministry of Culture and Islamic Guidance (MCIG).

Yet writers seem to ignore the impact of Neshat's milieu of exposure to cinema and galleries within New York, fast to credit her influences firmly within Iranian film generally and the work of Abbas Kirostami particularly. While that influence is accurate (Neshat also credits filmmakers Rakhshan Bani-Etemad and Mohsen Makhmalbaf), it reduces the intercultural position of her filmmaking, resulting from diasporic flows of films and filmmakers worldwide to Euro-American metropolises. Characterized by the experimentation apt to be shown in museums and galleries, such films "represent the experience of living between two or more cultural regimes of knowledge" and the "disjunctions in space and time [of] the diasporic experience." It is to this latter condition that entails "representing memory… through an appeal to nonvisual, embodied knowledge" from which a more complete understanding of Neshat's work arises and resists cultural representation.[19]

Film theorists and historians, from Barthes to Iles, have described cinema as the 'black box.' Seductive and entrancing, it promotes passive viewing of an illusionistic world-on-screen, whereas the 'white cube' of the museum or gallery is idealized as a space of criticality and active viewing. This assumed differentiation stems from Bellour's cinema-situation, within which the conditions that are both filmic (mis-en-scene, narrative, cinematography, etc.) and spatial (darkened space, sustained sitting with others) will suspend viewers in time and space, permitting an experience of perception and memory. However, it is the nature of the film that encourages either wholesale consumption of the images presented or the "pensive spectator" – that is, the viewer activated in an intellectual consideration of the film.[20] Visitors to the white cube entered a less hypnotic situation; aware of film as apparatus, the presence of projection eschewed illusion and emphasized experimentation with media. Even the physicality of movement versus sitting requires more physical and intellectual autonomy. However, projected-image works within the white cube are not entirely exclusionary of popular cinema practices, and exhibitions of the late 1990s will largely abandon monitors and machinery as explicit media within the viewer's space to the imperceptibly quiet digital projector's virtualizing effect. Balsom and Tamara Trodd determine that assigning strictly differentiated categories of viewer engagement between cinema and gallery is problematic, and Bellour expanded his theories of embodiment and cinema to the gallery space by the end of the 1990s.

It is with the virtualizing effect that we can trace the cinematic turn within museums and galleries, trending toward the spectacle nature of exhibition practices to which moving-image installations would play a major role. Balsom notes the economic factors at play within museums' "experience economy," under which institutions are not objective spaces of criticality but driven by the practicalities of economics/funding and the expectation to both maintain and create cultural relevancies.[21] She cites Rosalind Krauss, who in the late 1990s noted the challenges facing museums to attract audiences and procure funds, and how these challenges influenced exhibition practices that could be met by public interest in new technologies and the experiential.[22] The possibilities for the projected image to meet these demands was predicated by the phenomenological emphases of Minimalism as a precursor to artists' concerns with the spatial environment of viewership.

It is then understandable that Neshat often described her video works as "sculptural" and "minimal," converging the veiled bodies of her black-and-white films to her visual experiences of Iran in the early 1990s, an atmosphere she further described as devoid of color. Black-and-white also best suited an exaggeration of opposing dynamics in her narrative sequences. The virtualizing immersivity of projected images/video installations, met with high-fidelity sound and high-gloss visuality, dislocate space with media technologies to imbricate memory and identity at a newly embodied site. As with her photographs, the narrative fragments of Neshat's video installations intersect numerous cultural, social, and philosophical issues, bearing the failures of representation and history to adequately contain the complexities of memory and identity. It was a fertile environment for Neshat to initiate her own approaches to the postmodern critique of representation and curatorial interests in the cinematic turn, reconstituting the latter with the coordinates of a psychological geography necessary to efface the oversimplifications of diaspora and memory, exile and longing.

Turbulent

Following the completion of her vision of a woman running through the streets, Neshat sought to present a woman achieving independence from the repressive mediations of culture. *Turbulent* (Figure 2.3) was her first work shot in black-and-white film and the first in a trilogy of dual-screen projections. Neshat retained the centrality of an isolated female subject, yet furthered spatial interaction by situating two competing projections for the discursive placement of the viewer in active contemplation. The use of dual-screen projection called upon the viewer's own physical and sensory shifts within the viewing space, and such physical awareness demanded active investment in the images and actions before them. Jones's "intersubjectivity" and Bellour's "cinema-situation" are necessary for understanding Neshat's deft consideration of the viewing space, drawing subject and viewer into a single embodied space that disarms exotic readings.

The viewer teases out the opposing narratives in *Turbulent* relationally to one another, projected upon opposite walls in the darkened space. On one, a man sings a traditional poem by Jalal al-Din Muhammad Rumi (1207–73), the famous poet and Sufi mystic of the thirteenth-century. Performed by filmmaker Shoja Azari, he fervently lip syncs the beautiful singing of famed traditional Iranian vocalist, Shahram Nazeri. He sings facing the viewer, filling the frame in half-portrait with an audience of similarly clothed men behind him. At the song's end, he turns to bow to his audience of men in white shirts and, taking note of the sounds emerging from the opposite screen, returns to half-portrait view. Standing between, the viewer is mitigated into the action and space of interpretive exchange. At the moment Azari ceases performing, he turns his gaze toward the viewers' space. By way of that field of vision, he imbricates them with the woman on the opposite screen, the source of the new sound.

If the profound silences within her photographs imbue the images with meaning, then Neshat's *Turbulent* is a primal scream. Motionless with her back to the camera, a discordant and emotive sound begins to emanate from her cloaked form. She sings in an identical auditorium but for no one; the seats are empty, referencing Iran's law against public performances by women. Isolated, the singer is allowed to improvise and create new forms of sound that in their liberated quality achieve a greater level of transcendence and spirituality than the traditional poetry and music of the privileged group of men. During her song, the man stands steadfastly looking toward the opposite screen, his expression could be read as confusion or awe. But only he, the other artist, seems to recognize the significance of the woman's vocalization; the men in his audience appear largely unimpressed. Others are so obscured and motionless as to be indecipherable, anonymous men who perhaps cannot hear and are therefore excluded from the experience.

The singer is played by Sussan Deyhim, an Iranian composer based in New York and known for experimental combinations of technology with Persian traditional music and intense vocalizations. In her composition for the video, Deyhim's voice swells from a deep, soft alto and rises in a fervent crescendo of shrill noise. Also included is a kind of *ululation*, a

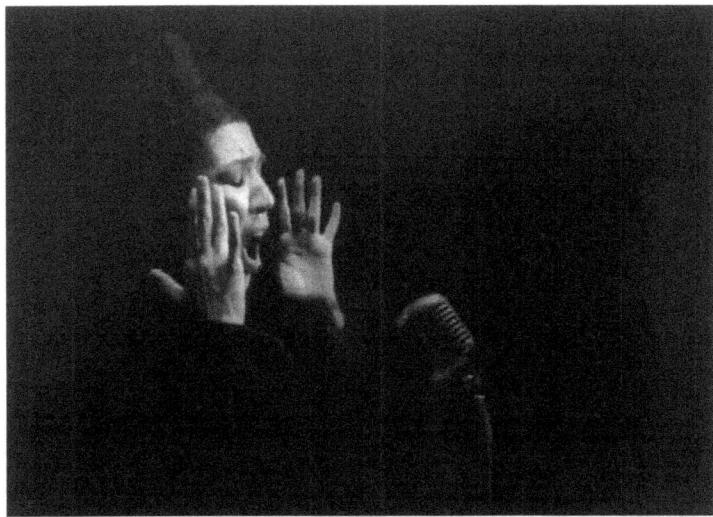

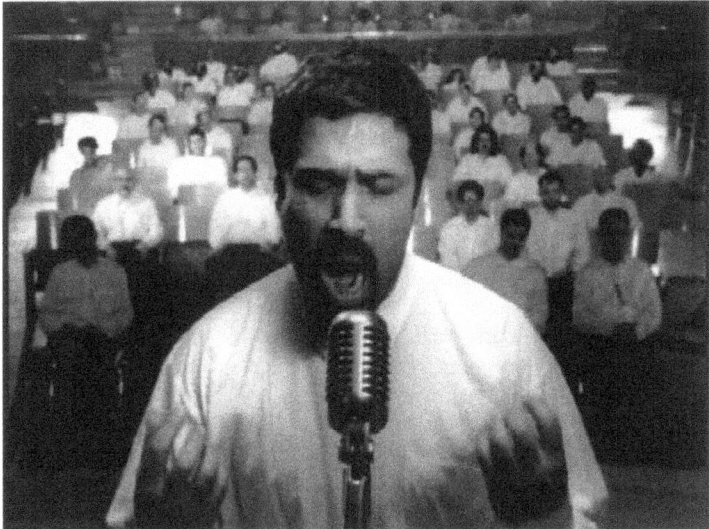

Figure 2.3 (a, b) Turbulent, 1998. Film Stills. © Shirin Neshat. Courtesy of the artist
and Gladstone Gallery,

traditional technique of Muslim women in celebration or mourning. As her
song becomes hurried and louder the camera spins around her, referencing as
in *Anchorage* the whirling dervish dance, the height of meditative commun-
ion with God among Mevlevi Sufis. Her long black cloak is recognizable as

chador but her headdress is similar to the *sikke*, the Sufi's woolen hat representing a headstone symbolic of the death of the ego through the dance. Eventually, Deyhim's composition and voice are amplified, enveloping the viewer.

Again, it is sound rather than speech that shapes memory from audial textures, an intersubjective recognition that goes beyond direct translation of experience to its sensory notations. Theories of performativity since the 1970s position viewership as more immediately brought into the present/presence of an acting subject on view, while screen theory concomitantly emphasized the seductive nature of subjects in cinematic form, the psychoanalytic or semiotic meanings below the surface. These theories coalesce in the cinematic installation space of Neshat's work in which, to apply Marks's understanding, "temporal immediacy, a co-presence, between viewer and object" goes beyond "looking at a representation to an experience in line with physical contact."[23] This adheres to Bellour's cinema-body that comprised of both the film-body and the spectator-body, enjoined by purely sensorial effects within their situational space. The temporal procedure of that space, and the affective content the filmic media renders, further reactivate memory as embodied perceptions that rely upon phenomenology to open subjectivity as a mutually created endeavor of spectator and subject, what Marks calls the "self in-becoming" (spectator) and its "embodied intercessor" (cinema). If "spectatorship is the sensory translation of cultural knowledge,"[24] in *Turbulent* the viewer's perception is conditioned by specificities of the film's circumstances yet transported into the subject's isolation, injustice, and transcendence via sound and spatial dynamics in the viewing situation.

The demands imposed onto the viewer via the in-between position of the installation mimics Neshat's own transnational subjectivity, a perspective affected by two worlds. In the brochure that accompanied *Turbulent* in its 1998 exhibition at the Whitney Museum, Neery Melkonian suggests that the woman's creative gesture constitutes the "third space" from which the viewer may understand diasporic experience. But physically the third space is that of the viewer, and the work's primary theme is the tension between oppositional approaches to spirituality and creativity to emphasize how societal laws can equally repress both male and female subjects. The woman can never perform in public; the man can achieve fame and recognition but can never attain her creativity and spiritual awareness. It is significant that the largely Euro-American audience of this piece recognize Deyhim's song as improvised sounds but are unlikely to understand the words by Rumi. This creates a communicative obstruction bearing similarity with Neshat's photographs in which words remain mysterious. The recognition of foreign imagery and signs give way to a recognition that emotive, original expression is more powerful than collective, traditional approaches.

Although the Sufis are a spiritual group who seek an individualized union with God that could be described as "mystical," the basis of their religious vocabulary comes from Arabic as well as Islamic sources. In Turkey, women can participate in the whirling dervish dance of the Mevlevis, which is viewed as a performance of cultural heritage. But it is banned for both men and women in Mohammad's home of Saudi Arabia as well as Iran, where Sufi leaders are regarded as "an unacceptable alternative spiritual authority" to the dominant religious clerics.[25] Contrasting the song of the Rumi poem, which is about divine love, with a freely improvised performance, highlights the strict regulation of Persian cultural heritage, wherein the popularity of Rumi's poems cannot be dismissed or censored but his philosophies regarding an individual path to Allah often are. Her marginalized position allows the female performer to take risks and attain the truth of Rumi's teachings.

"Turbulent" perhaps best describes the work's varying sounds and motions, and the tension between the two worlds of the male and female performers. One is a mainstream interpretation of a spiritual, albeit popular poem that satisfies the audience in an aggrandizing moment for the performer, while the other is an intensely wrought excavation of the self, freed from the limitations of public acceptance. Melkonian compared the tension between lyrics and abstract sounds in the work to the differences between the sacred love of Rumi's poem and the profane love of the woman's desperate indecipherability.[26] This "transcendence of the written word" inherent in the woman's sound can be transgressive for the viewer as well, witness to her primal and erotic energy. However, the creation of her work is only made possible through the freedom of her social marginalization, the outcast status of the exile.

I have attempted to frame that, despite the unfamiliar content of the piece, it's difficult for particularly the female spectator to maintain the distance necessary for Brechtian criticality alone. This further problematizes the cinema/passive and museum/active categories because simultaneous operations that are sensorial, emotional, critical, and seductive take place within its embodied viewing. Even without knowledge of Iran's laws against female participation in public performance, one gleans prohibition based on gender from the woman's isolation, and the inherent knowledge of the desirability placed upon the female body as the source of her marginalization. The viewers' embodied relation to Deyhim detaches them from the simplistic voyeurism inherent to performance, mitigating their distance to the desired as an "intensified relation with an Other that cannot be possessed." Neshat seduces us "through a desiring and often pleasurable relationship to the image" that Marks further estimates as a physical, or erotic, spectatorship that "closes the distance and implicates the viewer in the viewed."[27]

The connectivities between voyeur and viewed, erotic object and embodied subject, draw a route back to preoccupations with mysticism and repression in *Turbulent*. The erotic nature of both is the basis for Michel Foucault's *A Preface to Transgression* (1963), arguably marking the beginning of his larger body of work dedicated to the relationship between knowledge and power and how their expressions are used to objectivize particularly marginalized subjects whose individualities society seeks to repress. As he puts forth in his essay, spirituality or a path to the divine has been described in terms such as desire, rapture, ecstasy, only possible by crossing a boundary from procreative sexuality to eroticism, from sacred to profane. Foucault challenged established functions of boundary and taboo, positing "the limit" between self and culture that can only be illuminated by its crossing *and* recrossing, a fluidity that produces subjectivity through interaction with the limit. Deyhim's exalted sounds go beyond the limit of traditional song, an excessive, erotically charged originality, in which we witness

> transgression [that] prescribes not only the sole manner of discovering the sacred in its unmediated substance, but a way of recomposing its absence ... where all our actions are addressed to this absence in a profanation which at once identifies, dissipates, exhausts itself in it, and restores it to the purity of its transgression.[28]

Transgression as 'pure' occurs in the space where subjectivities at the margins do not transgress boundaries or limits as much as they self-actualize through destabilization of the limits, as it "opens this zone to existence for the first time... immobilized in scenes we call 'erotic' and volatized in a philosophical turbulence."[29]

Rapture

Neshat's next dual-screen projection, *Rapture* (1999) (Figure Intro.1) focuses on groups of men and women in opposition, a collective experience rather than a singular one. The men are publicly determined, occupying the space of architecture while the women reside in the space of nature. A medieval fortress contains the men in their identical white shirts, juxtaposed against women in chador traversing a desert setting near the sea on the opposite screen. Separate but connected, their movements and actions appear choreographed as the work progresses. The hierarchically elevated world of the men in their fortress is destabilized by the egalitarian freedom of the women as they gather on the beach lying beyond its walls. The corridors of the fortress, which Neshat and her team scouted for its Islamic character, seem to constrict the crowd of men in opposition to the openness of space afforded to the women.

Shot in Essaouira, Morocco, the fortress may be generically perceived as belonging to a place and time rooted in the past. The large groups of men and women in the composition demanded various aerial shots that place the human forms against built and natural environments, creating an effect Neshat has referred to as "sculptural," yet an ambitiously sophisticated use of architecture and landscape. While the men perform vague tasks that fuse them together in a mass, the women wander freely and dispersed.

An accompanying soundtrack by Deyhim underscores the movements on each screen, dividing and directing the viewer's focus. For the men there is a driving, pulsating rhythm corresponding to their forceful actions and for the women a dissonant and lyrical melody accentuates the fluidity of their walk across the sand. The men move quickly through the corridors and over the parapets, raising ladders to speed their ascent. But their efforts result in an absurd series of actions, and eventually they wrestle and fight among themselves in chaos. Finally, their attention is diverted from their impotent struggles by the ululations of the women who have converged in the desert landscape. Silently the men watch the women raise their ritual cry.

In its traditional Middle Eastern and Arabic usage, ululation can be interpreted in multiple ways: as applause, celebration, sadness, or warning. Here it has the sense of intervention as the camera scans the women who look directly at the viewer as well as upwards toward the heights of the fortress. As they ululate, they reveal Persian texts written across their palms; potential interpretation would be hindered by their brevity on-screen, and therefore they equally import inscription upon their bodies. As with her photographs, texts suggest the bodily relationship to memory and language as sign systems that are condensed and translated into visual form. Yet in some cultural traditions of Islam, text is written upon the hands in commemoration of religious festival and the women may have come together for such purpose.[30] The wall of the fortress may be a symbol of Islam itself, tying it to the qibla wall of a mosque; the men in the fortress wash, also indicative of preparation for prayer. But these interpretations are mimetic traces assumed and bound up in the criteria of Islam, Persian literature, even Conceptual Art, and dissipate under a multiplicity of signs.

Both groups eventually convene in a circle, but rather than submit in prayer the men engage in vaguely administrative activities; their circle is a council where they gesture at each other argumentatively. At this point the final stage of the narrative takes shape as the women turn away from the massive walls of the fortress, hence religion or authority, while bound to it the men are unable to leave. A single woman pounds a drum with her feet, and this change in the film's score signals a call to the women to rise and move across the barren landscape toward the sea. At the conclusion, several of the women push a boat across the beach onto the waves, and with the help of an outboard motor make their way beyond the horizon.

Neshat's inspiration for the narrative of *Rapture* comes again from Persian literature. *Ahl-i-gharq (someone who would be brave enough to drown)* is a 1989 novel by writer Moniru Ravani'pur in which a small village is flooded. While the men run in fear, the women dance and drum, praying to Allah to stop the waters and spare the children. As the boat continues across the horizon in *Rapture*, the concluding image depicts the men in the fortress waving, some with both arms, standing atop the parapets. Whether a gesture of farewell or a cry for help is not clear. Whether the women motor away as a willful act of liberation is also not clear. Despite narrative ambiguities, the rich black-and-white film accentuates the textures and stark simplicity of the groups' uniform clothing, gray fortress, and open vistas of water and desert. The distant chadors moving across the sand, shrouding the individual identities as they splay out across the beach, emphasize the independent nature of the women in contrast to the men, who huddle together behind great stone walls.

Rapture appeared in many exhibitions after its release in 1999. In the exhibition guide for its premier at the Art Institute of Chicago, curator James Rondeau noted that the women's journey from the desert to the sea is parallel to the migration of those who have voluntarily left their homeland.[31] And yet the austere setting of the desert and the image of veiled women, a dress rooted in ancient tradition, connect the image to religious exodus narratives. As the strength of the women unfolds, the repression is made evident in their need to escape. As with all diasporas, not everyone is liberated or has the desire to leave. The fate of those who flee and those who remain intertwine, if only in the psychological connections between memory and loss that are bound to the diasporic experience. In the fortress, the men are associated with modernity and culture, even conflict. In the space of the desert and the sea, the women are associated with nature and freedom. Much like *Turbulent*, the men are restricted to societal norms while the women invent a new solution.

In this space, of both the film and its viewing, new knowledge is generated from and between cultures, to the backdrop of Foucault's purity of transgression that occurs in crossing and recrossing the limit. This is evident in film's essential relationship to memory that occurs, according to Marks, in its movement "backward and forward in time, inventing histories and memories to posit an alternative to the overwhelming erasures, silences, and lies of official history." Neshat participates in this process that Marks describes, dismantling and reconstituting "the traces of collective life that inform the structure of perception."[32] As a diasporic artist, *Rapture* is neither representative of life in Iran nor its memory, but an alternative to the gaps and fissures of memory created by separation, isolation, and personal perspective. Further, history is bound to layers of images that are public (film, media) and wrestle against "the unpreserved present-that-passes" as the unofficial history of private memories.[33] It is this acutely complex sense of memory by which Toni Morrison realized she could not trust recorded history and understood the paradox of remembering and forgetting necessary "to carve out a world both culture specific and 'race-free.'" Neshat's films also posit the contradictions of "memory and memorylessness" to reach for culturally specific images and content and yet transgress their limitations as a Muslim woman straddling two different perceptual worlds.[34]

Careful not to assume authority or engage in a "culture totalizing process," Morrison's "rememory" is central to her writing that involved the deconstruction and reconstruction of memory toward new knowledge and meaning, in this case of our collective legacy of slavery: "For imaginative entrance into that territory I urged memory to metamorphose itself into metaphorical and imagistic associations." Filled with imagistic associations and ambiguity, it is particularly the women in *Rapture* who fill the psychic space of the viewer in a deconstruction/reconstruction of existing reality, resisting societies in which "they are spoken of and written about – objects of history, not subjects within it." Morrison invented a new textual structure better serving the experience of her characters who must live in "a system in which the conquerors write the narrative of their lives."[35] It is to this latter statement that Neshat's films, and the physical viewership of their installation, also seek alternatives for viewer and subject viewed, lying beyond limitations and impositions, 'recomposing' the established narrative's 'empty form,' and culling a 'usable past' toward liberational meaning.

Embodied Subjects in Moving-Images

Incongruity and inconsistency converge in the rememory of a history denied to Neshat in exile and presented to her as sign through mediated images in the US. She accordingly destabilizes the viewer's knowledge, both of self and other, beyond the limits of representation and relationship to screen. Rememory as postmodern literary analysis is not far-removed considering that "enunciation" is one way film scholars understand filmic point-of-view, cultivated by an "auteur" who uses images as a kind of writing.[36] Neshat's split-screen projection format effectively places the viewer within a "strategically perspectival milieu"[37] in which the viewer is physically positioned to make interpretive leaps. Though the narratives of the men and women are rendered independently in their physical separation on two screens, they are irrevocably related and synchronized by gazes, music, and the cause-and-effect rhythm of their actions. This blend of relative meaning resulting from subjective, interactive viewing of the familiar-yet-unknown requires consideration beyond stereotyped representation. No longer caricatures of the Islamic East, the women in *Turbulent* and *Rapture* are capable of agency and liberation, no longer determined by the constrictions the spectator of space, religion, and male authority in Neshat's reimagined spaces.

These spaces include both the locational and contextual sites of her films and the situational space of the viewer in the work's totality as video installation. I addressed earlier the problems with monolithically assigning passive spectatorship to cinema and active criticality to exhibition in the viewing situation. The nature of video, whether on monitor or projected, may concomitantly incite the individual or 'flâneur' ambling about in an exhibition, while there is a seated/sited demand upon the cinema's collective audience. Bellour's outline of elements that constitute the cinema-situation and engage a "pensive spectator" is, as he stressed, contingent upon the nature of the film and the ways it enacts upon the viewer. Neshat's approach, positioning a polished cinematic work within a practice of installation, and the dependent choreographed nature of the dueling projections, demands attentiveness toward movement in relationship to the screens in a duration of roughly ten minutes. The preference among artists for millimeter film as a nostalgic medium, hybridized to digitization and DVD transfer in the transitory space of the museum/gallery white cube also imbued the work with cultural and historical value. These conditions undergirded the "cinematic turn" of contemporary exhibitions, combining the spectacle of moving-images with the temporal/spatial experience of viewing an artwork.

Emphasis on the 'architecture' that shapes viewing begins with Sheldon Renan's 'expanded cinema' and on to the writings of Bellour, Jean-Christophe Royoux, and Giuliana Bruno. For Royoux, the cinematic turn lies in the hybridization of the material conditions in both actual and narrative spaces of the moving-image. Bruno emphasizes the spectator and 'site-seeing' as the physical analogy for cinema's ability to serve as "an agent of intersubjective and cultural memory," its proximity and presence in the exhibition context collapsing distance in physically and cognitively immersive ways.[38] Arising from these new spectatorial relations to the moving-image are theories of embodiment that can be traced to Maurice Merleau-Ponty's problematization of 'the visual' as something differentiated and distanced from the spectator. Joanna Lowry has noted that faces projected large and in proximity before us "address not only the disengaged spectator of modernist tradition, but an object of the gaze produced by the image" and that in these "contemporary video installations we are no longer positioned as objective observers [but] positioned instead as embodied spectators." The physical convergence of the gaze and the quasi-theatre of the gallery facilitate a cognitive relationship between image, spectator, and "dialogic space." Within this temporal/spatial experience, mediated by a technological apparatus, the dialogic relationship between spectator and subject emphasizes the "modern self" as a "set of symptoms" that are psychological and cultural.[39] Returning to Walsh's "entrancement," video installations such as Neshat's "foreground medium at the expense of narrative" while using familiar cinematic "means of producing pleasure and encouraging identification" that "generates a psycho-physiological diffusion in the viewer."[40]

Merleau-Ponty and Luce Irigaray have both noted that the rhythmic propulsions of song and poetry exemplify affectivity, and Lowry and Walsh also take note of rhythm and movement in temporal suspension of the spectator before moving-image works. Although Irigaray cautioned against Merleau-Ponty's privileging of vision, they both recognized the important climax of embodied perception occurring when the viewer relinquishes power over the viewed, allowing a mimetic or intersubjective relationship that Marks positions as a "phenomenological model of subjectivity" based on "the mutual creation of self and other." The psycho-physiological imbrication, alongside the affective rhythms of sound and movement, supersedes the alterity of Neshat's subjects and one's own culturally determined self and its "set of symptoms." In her response to Merleau-Ponty, Irigaray's embodiment investigates "the most general and universal features of perceptual experience" an essential component of which is temporal and reflexive toward "double sensation" of "self-other" that, in its most empathic sense, "can identify with the other's living body in its movement and expression."[41]

Embodiment and performativity, their emphasis on the corporeal, are fundamental to both gender and post-colonial studies. Neshat's constructions of gendered subjectivity at the intersections of history, religion, and politics in the post-revolutionary period imbricate – through the embodied and entrancing relationship described – an empathic and ethical viewership. As film made its way into the white cube and moving-image installation became more immersive, spectators were made "fragmented, intermittent" by a destabilized viewing experience that film had hitherto offered them as a familiar medium.[42] Neshat's dual-screen projections rely on the viewer to embody the formal devices of the camera, such as shot/reverse shot; without those obvious markers to direct the eye, the viewer is both fragmented and activated, shaken from complacency. Once the ten-minute experience ends and the viewer disembarks from its illusory conditions, returning from the limit they confront what Foucault called the

> tearing of the subject from itself in such a way that it is no longer the subject as such, or that it is completely 'other' … so that it may arrive at its dissociation… a 'limit-experience' that tears the subject from itself.

It is in this tearing, within the temporal and discursive realm of an aesthetic (of) experience, as Caroline A. Jones and Marsha Meskimmon have observed, that transformation may evolve into a responsible/response-able viewership, the potential for Foucault's limit-experience as a collective practice.[43]

Fervor

Neshat's final installation of her trilogy, *Fervor* (2000) (Figure 2.4) looks at individual experience *within* the collective and with the most structured narrative. In another dual-screen projection, *Fervor* manipulates camera angles align the actions occurring on both screens. This side-by-side, mirrored projection is arguably the most complex of the trilogy visually, yet effectively emphasizes its male and female protagonists in the same physical and psychological space. The viewer is activated in following both projections simultaneously to "acquire the continuity that conventional cinema provides via the pushy consolation of montage."[44] On separate screens, a woman and a man walk down a dusty road across the same barren expanse of land. Eventually, they meet at the intersection of their dirt roads, but always projected on separate screens. They pause before continuing along their paths, but they are seen again entering the same space.

Men in modern white shirts and dark pants and women in chador are again contrasted with each other in the space of a single meeting hall. They have convened before an orator, perhaps a *mullah* (religious leader) or a politician. A long black curtain cuts the space lengthwise, separating the men and women on the opposite screens. The man and woman take their seats on either side, noticing one another once more and realizing that they have arrived at the same place. From the raised stage, the speaker recites the story of Yusuf and Zulaikha, one of the most popular stories from the Qur'an and a parable of temptation and sins of the flesh.

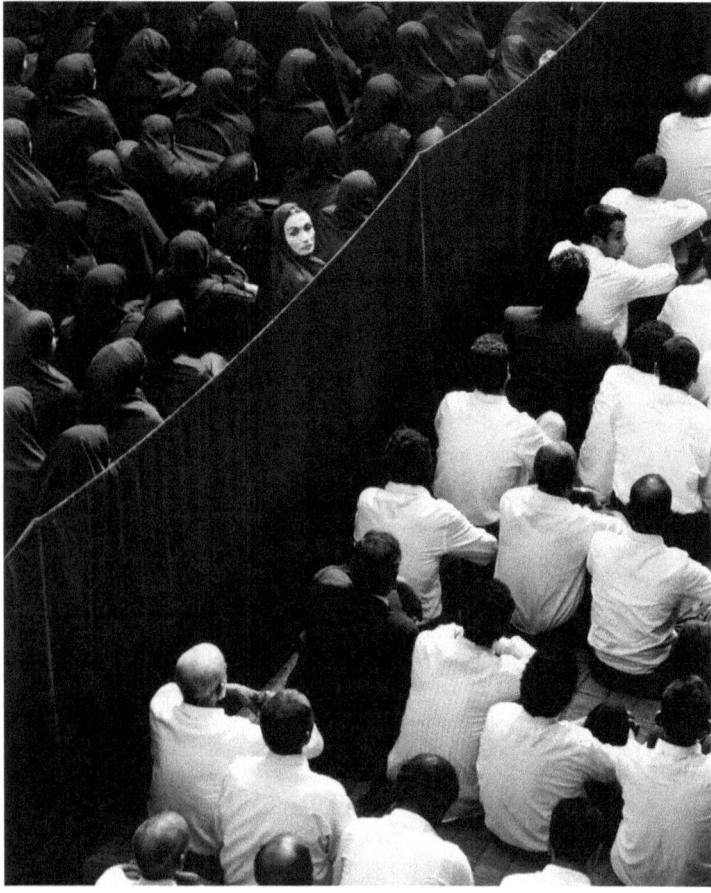

Figure 2.4 Fervor, 2000. Film Still (photo by Larry Barns). © Shirin Neshat. Courtesy of the artist and Gladstone Gallery.

Sexuality was an issue Neshat intended to address when she began planning the three consecutive videos. Her partner and collaborator, Shoja Azari, wrote the script for *Fervor*, a plot that most directly emphasizes the commonality of desire in both men and women. The man's spoken word underscores a narrative current, although *Fervor* was presented without subtitles, retaining the work's ambiguity. Even if the viewer cannot understand Persian, they can sense the moral authority the speaker commands. The man and woman look with longing to the curtain that separates them, and the tension of their proximity to one another is intensified by the orator's fervent speech. The audience responds to his caution against sexual temptation with ululations and cries that seem to validate his authority and the story's moral. Silent and overwhelmed, the woman flees while the man remains confined within the space of conformity. As in *Rapture*, her flight is ambiguous: whether she leaves in defiance and rebellion, or shame and fear is unclear.

The force of the orator's authority and the acceptance of his word by the audience suppress the feelings between the man and woman, inferring the encroachment of society's repression on individual choice. Veiled women are further charged with the culpability of desire precisely because they have been given the responsibility of concealment. According to Ayatollah Morteza Motahhari, who blueprinted Iran's Veiling Act, this culpability is substantiated with women for whom "the desire to show off and display oneself is a particular trait." For his successor, Ayatollah Ali Meshkini, "Looking is rape by means of the eyes."[45] Citing Freud, Naficy also proposes that lack of male/female contact and the closure of the female body only increase desire because distance is the necessary component to the scopophilic pleasure of looking.[46] This is heightened by the juxtaposition of long shots and close-ups of the players' faces, enhancing recognition of the gaze and its relationship to longing.

The soft sounds of a woman's voice that comprise the background are performed by Deyhim, and sound is again an important unifying element. Although *Fervor* has the strongest connection to the spoken word in the trilogy, the contrasting silence between the two protagonists is apparent. The Islamic tale of Yusuf and Zulaikha replace Neshat's use of Persian prose, and the universality of its moral kinship with Christianity and Judaism are important to the work's universal message. The married Zuleikha's attempt to seduce Yusef, her husband's favorite servant, reveals her as a sinner. Yusef's ability to deny her out of respect for his master, evincing respect for Allah, reveals him as holy. According to Mernissi, it is a gendering of morality by which women are considered potentially destructive to the Muslim social order.[47] However, the position of women to public and political space in Iran is more urgent and to which the veil ensures that women remain unseen and unheard.

Deborah Solomon observed that it was difficult to view Neshat's trilogy without having a political reaction: "they are always reminding you that Iran is a repressive place where a woman must cloak her body."[48] Understood through Enlightenment concepts, the work was often narrowly interpreted as a critique of Islamic-Iranian society that reinforced Western feminist values. Neshat was aware of such potential interpretations, although acutely sensitive to essentialism, of pandering to Western audiences curious about Middle East culture. Using Penny Florence's phrase, the "sexed universal" of Neshat's art, and perhaps any female artist of color or from non-Western countries, is that she is sought as an interlocutor for understanding an identity made already-exotic by centers of curation that replace colonialism in their presentation and discourse of these territories. Thereby, the female body is reinscribed as a kind of territory, one that artists from Mendieta to Neshat reclaim at the limits. Amna Malik has noted that the work of diasporic Iranian women-artists interrogates spatiality and "brings spectatorship into connection with the body and its movement ... and which colonialism has marked as territories possessed."[49] Breaking past the boundary between viewer/viewed, self/other, Neshat employs cultural generalities that tap into sensorial memories of isolation, repression, and liberation. It is especially a female-identifying spectator to these works who translate via these equivalencies regardless of her familiarity with their cultural specificities.

The Transnational's Double Transgression

However multi-layered Neshat's first trilogy, I have attempted to address Iranian socio-political and religious history embedded in its themes. To be transnational, by definition, is to doubly transgress. By offering liberatory female subjects through the deployment of ostensibly Conceptual Art and installation practices – if we proceed from a Western epistemology of avant-gardism – Neshat defies the Islamic State. She also transgresses the West by invoking the politics of Islam in a reflexive turn, re-presenting the other to reveal ourselves to ourselves in an embodied subjectivity, where one may recognize religion and the nation-state as oppressive forces upon gendered realities and individual freedom across cultures. Reflexivity emerges from Walsh's entranced or hypnotic state "whereby the subject is possessed by a strangeness" that comes from a "zone of experience normally unattended to in which borders between self and other, constituting an incommunicable *lived experience*" activate embodied viewing. Following Georges Bataille to Mikkel Borch-Jacobsen, who posit the importance of entrancement and its affective criteria to an experience of "being-other," reflexivity is yet tempered by the suggestibility of individual viewers. Embodiment begins with the premise that all bodies are inscribed with their own cultural, psychological, and physical meanings, simultaneously making use of and problematizing "universality" as a "visceral immediacy."[50] Sense perceptions, if they are understood to precede before these meanings, still "allow for, and indeed require, the mediation of memory" toward the intersubjectivity of mutual recognition.[51]

Neshat's work fit the experience economy of biennials and museums, spectacle exhibitions and cinematic installations, spaces whose additional goal was the global refashioning of a new world view and recognized her work as the epitome of "universality." Often reductive binary summations of its themes – East/West, male/female, religion/secularism, culture/nature – were pursuant from center/periphery understandings characteristic of the era of multiculturalism. A more complex interpretation of Neshat's operative binaries was offered by Hamid Dabashi's essay for *Women of Allah* (1997). He described the collective gazes of the series' subjects as "mocking" both the patriarchal and the colonial, "pitting them against each other" until they eventually collapse under Neshat's "visual strategy."

> That kind of gaze is only possible from the transgressive site of a New York state of imagination, a no-man's land, as it were, of migratory dreams. The immigrant artist, or the photographer in exile ... She can never fully function as the integral force from "within" a society.[52]

Fastening Neshat's strategy to her physical and mental location as a transcultural experience of living among people from across the globe, Dabashi perhaps most accurately assessed her identity, cultivated with her practice as a third view "engaging a dialogue with a culture or two, with no immediate audience in either and yet something profoundly important to say to both."

Turbulent was entered into the 1999 Venice Biennale and awarded the Golden Lion, the exhibition's First International Prize. The attention was indicative of the evolution of curatorial practices over the last decade, moving from representation to a third space of liminal identities as indicated by Homi Bhabha, and the authoritative role of the audience via emphasis on experience and interaction as suggested by Francesco Bonami. Neshat's video installations appeared responsive to Bhabha's "third space" as a territory for suspension and negotiation of fixed identities and Bonami's directive to turn viewers into participants in the work of art. Impacted by the 1999 Biennale, Bellour maintained cinema's distance from contemporary art while recognizing the growing significance of the "unfamiliar, endlessly mutating" forms of time-based/moving-image installations. Their models of spectatorship promoted the pensive-engaged (cognitive) and embodied (affective) viewer and anticipated the urgency to reimagine subjectivity in an intensely globalized world.

Notes

1 Jones, Amelia. "Televisual Flesh: Activating otherness in New Media Art." *Parachute*, no. 113 (Winter 2004), p. 71–91.
2 Mulvey, Laura. *Death 24x a Second: Stillness and the Moving Image*. London: Reaktion Books, 2006.

3 Radner, Hilary. "Cinema and the Body: The Ghost in the Theater," in Radner, Hilary and Alistair Fox, eds. *Raymond Bellour: Cinema and the Moving Image* (Edinburgh: Edinburgh University Press, 2018), p. 52-69. It is translated from Bellour's *The Body of Cinema: Hypnoses, Emotions, Animalities*, (Paris: POL, 2009). The concept is also discussed in Maria Walsh's "You've Got Me Under Your Spell: The Entranced Spectator." Trodd, Tamara eds. *Screen/Space: The Projected Image in Contemporary Art*. (Manchester: Manchester University Press, 2011), p. 113.

4 Balsom, Erika. *Exhibiting Cinema in Contemporary Art*. Amsterdam: Amsterdam University Press, 2013. p. 11.

5 MacDonald, Scott. "Between Two Worlds: An Interview with Shirin Neshat." *Feminist Studies*, vol. 30, no. 3. (Fall, 2004). p. 630.

6 Marks, Laura U. *The Skin of the Film: Intercultural Cinema, Embodiment, and the Senses*. Durham: Duke University Press, 2000. p. 140.

7 Zaya, Octavio. "Q&A Shirin Neshat: Islamic Women as Ambiguous Icons." *Creative Camera* (Oct./Nov. 1996). p. 18.

8 Balsom, Erika. *Exhibiting Cinema in Contemporary Art*, p. 11.

9 Naficy, Hamid. "Phobic Spaces and Liminal Panics: Independent Transnational Film Genre." Wilson, Rob and Wimal Dissanayake eds. *Global/Local: Cultural Production and the Transnational Imaginary*. Durham: Duke University Press, 1996. (119–144). p. 120.

10 Neshat, Shirin. MFA Thesis Exhibition Statement (Aug., 1982). University of Berkeley Art Museum & Pacific Film Archive.

11 MacDonald, Scott. "Between Two Worlds: An Interview with Shirin Neshat." p. 631.

12 Leleu, Natalie. "The Image Dispute." *Parachute* no. 100 (October–December, 2000). p. 80. Bonami, Francesco. "The Shadow Under the Web." *Women of Allah*. Turin: Marco Norie Editions, 1997.

13 Ibid.

14 Leventis, Andreas. "Home Truths: Three Middle-Eastern Artists Probe the Facts Behind the Fiction." *Modern Painters* (May 2006). p. 91.

15 Balsom, Erika. *Exhibiting Cinema in Contemporary Art*, p. 12.

16 Marks, Laura U. *The Skin of the Film: Intercultural Cinema, Embodiment, and the Senses*, p. 50.

17 Ibid.

18 Schad, Ed. *Shirin Neshat: I Will Greet the Sun Again*. New York: Delmonico-Prestel, 2020. p. 228.

19 Marks, Laura U. *The Skin of the Film: Intercultural Cinema, Embodiment, and the Senses*, p. 1–2.

20 Radner, Hilary and Alistair Fox trans. *Bellour, Raymond: Cinema and the Moving Image*. Edinburgh: Edinburgh University Press, p. 42.

21 Balsom, Erika. *Exhibiting Cinema in Contemporary Art*, p. 61.

22 Ibid., 19.

23 Marks, Laura U. *The Skin of the Film: Intercultural Cinema, Embodiment, and the Senses*, p. 140.

24 Ibid., p. 151–153.

25 Ernst, Carl. *Following Muhammad: Rethinking Islam in the Contemporary World*. Chapel Hill: University of North Carolina Press, 2003. p. 180.

26 Melkonian, Neery. "A Not-Yet-Named Third Space." *Shirin Neshat: Turbulent*. New York: Whitney Museum of American Art, 1998.

27 Marks, Laura U. *The Skin of the Film: Intercultural Cinema, Embodiment, and the Senses*, p. 184.

28 Bouchard, Donald trans. *Language, Counter-Memory, Practice: Selected Essays and Interviews of Michel Foucault*. Ithaca, NY: Cornell University Press, 1977. p. 30.

29 Ibid., 35 & 39.

30 Rondeau, James. *Shirin Neshat: Rapture.* Focus Exhibition Guide. The Art Institute of Chicago, 1999.

31 Ibid.

32 Marks, Laura U. *The Skin of the Film: Intercultural Cinema, Embodiment, and the Senses,* p. 24, 73.

33 Ibid., 41.

34 Morrison, Toni. "I Wanted to Carve Out a World Both Culturally Specific and Race-Free." *The Guardian* (Aug. 8, 2019).

35 Ibid.

36 Balsom, Erika. *Exhibiting Cinema in Contemporary Art,* p. 34.

37 Jones, Amelia. *Body Art: Performing the Subject.* Minneapolis: University of Minnesota Press, 1998. p. 40.

38 Uroskie, Andrew V. "Windows in the white cube." Trodd, Tamara eds. *Screen/Space: The Projected Image in Contemporary Art.* Manchester: Manchester University Press, 2011. p. 147.

39 Lowry, Joanna. "Projecting Symptoms." Trodd, Tamara ed. *Screen/Space: The Projected Image in Contemporary Art.* Manchester: Manchester University Press, 2011. p. 106 & 109.

40 Walsh, Maria. "'You've got me under your spell:' The Entranced Spectator," p. 113 & 119.

41 Lehtinen, Virpi. *Luce Irigaray's Phenomenology of Feminine Being.* Albany, NY: State University of New York Press, 2014. p. 55&57.

42 Balsom, Erika. *Exhibiting Cinema in Contemporary Art,* p. 55.

43 Jones, Caroline A. *The Global Work of Art.* Chicago: Chicago University Press, 2016. p. 222.

44 Horrigan, Bill. *Shirin Neshat: Two Installations.* New York: Distributed Art Publishers & The Wexner Center for the Arts, The Ohio State University, 2000. p. 13.

45 Afkhami, Mahnaz & Erika Friedl eds. *In the Eye of the Storm: Women in Post-Revolutionary Iran.* Syracuse, NY: Syracuse University Press, 1994, pp. 131–150. This is also discussed in Motahhari's *The Islamic Modest Dress,* 3rd ed. (Laleh Bakhtiar trans.) New York: Kazi Publications, 2007.

46 Naficy, Hamid. "Veiled Vision/Powerful Presences: Women in Post-Revolutionary Iranian Cinema." Afkhami, Mahnaz & Erika Friedl ed. *In the Eye of the Storm: Women in Post-Revolutionary Iran.* Syracuse, NY: Syracuse University Press, 1994.

47 Mernissi, Fatima. *Beyond the Veil: Male-Female Dynamics in Modern Muslin Society.* Bloomington, IN: Indiana University Press, 1987.

48 Solomon, Deborah. "Romance of the Chador." *New York Times Magazine,* (March 25, 2001). p. 40.

49 Malik, Amna. "Surface Tension: Reconsidering Horizontality in the Work of Diasporic Iranian Artists." Harris, Jonathan ed. *Identity Theft: The Cultural Colonization of Contemporary Art.* Liverpool University Press, 2008. p. 109–134, 111.

50 Walsh, Maria. "'You've got me under your spell:' The Entranced Spectator." Trodd, Tamara eds. *Screen/Space: The Projected Image in Contemporary Art.* Manchester: Manchester University Press, 2011. p. 114.

51 Marks, Laura U. *The Skin of the Film: Intercultural Cinema, Embodiment, and the Senses,* p. 145 & 147.

52 Dabashi, Hamid. "Shirin Neshat's Photography." *Shirin Neshat: Women of Allah.* Turin, Italy: Marco Noire Editions, 1997. Unpaginated.

3 'Here Vs. There'

Translation and the Global Exhibition

Neshat dropped her son at his school near Battery Park before heading to the editing studio on East Broadway on the morning of September 11, 2001. While walking along with Shoja Azari on Broome Street, they heard the first plane crash and saw smoke coming from the World Trade Center (WTC). After the second plane crash, they returned to the school to retrieve him, running through the streets.[1] Neshat had spent her career grappling with the social and cultural devastation of her native Iran and the disconnections between East/West. As an artist, Muslim, and New Yorker, her reaction to a terrorist attack, in her very neighborhood, was humanely articulated:

> Putting politics aside, just facing mortality to the degree I witnessed – seeing people fall out of the building and die in front of me – and seeing the building fall with my son, was apocalyptic... I felt an incredible sympathy for the people who lost their families. And yet, I am Iranian and my work has been totally dedicated, in a very minute way, to this conversation about the Western and Islamic conflict, in terms of contradictions that exist here versus there.[2]

This chapter investigates internationalism in art that cultivated "here versus there" and unravels its proclaimed characteristics, such as "universality." Although Neshat had consciously expressed universal emotions and experiences, "universalism" as a curatorial concept emerged problematically alongside exoticizing tendencies in international exhibition. There are profound shifts in her work from 2000 through 2002, an intensely short but prolific period impacted by 9/11 and her growing unease with critical and curatorial expectations placed on her as cultural representative. Indeed, it was a discourse surrounding Neshat's work, sutured to the cosmopolitan experience of globalism, that tended to exoticize Neshat under its demands for cultural representation and authenticity.

On 9/11, Neshat was about to edit video to be used in her first live performance piece, commissioned by The Kitchen. *The Conference of the Birds (Phase I)* was scheduled for September 21, then postponed in part due to

DOI: 10.4324/9781003341192-4

intensifying anti-Muslim sentiment after the attacks.[3] Based on the poem of the same name by twelfth-century Sufi Farid ud-Din Attar, it is an allegorical narrative of a quest undertaken by thousands of birds across the world in search of Simorgh, a king in the form of a flying chimera. The story evokes the Jewish exodus led by Moses and the doubts of Jesus's followers, symbolically drawing together disparate people into unified tribes seeking similar paths. Their journey begins with a chosen leader spiritually close to God, in this case, a female hoopoe, and it is made more difficult by her avian followers who complain and look for excuses to abandon the quest. In the week after 9/11, the work was altered from its original title to *The Logic of the Birds*, a change that may relate to the performance's emphasis on the birds' argumentation and in-fighting.

Neshat's video component was projected onto a screen behind the actors, who seem to emerge from screen to stage and back against her imagery of a dry landscape, sometimes apocalyptically burning under formidable mountains. By the end of Attar's poem, only 30 birds remain; *Si* (30) and *morgh* (bird) indicate that it was not a king they sought, but themselves as one people. The search for the divine and its relation to overcoming the ego of self in Sufism is supplanted by an allegorical quest of people who must understand their relations to one another, emphasizing community above the individual in Islamic culture. Played by Sussan Deyhim, the hoopoe retained centrality among the 30 players on stage. Attuned to the solitude and suffering necessary for the attainment of enlightenment, she "returns to a society that has become blinded, confused and has fallen into a state of chaos..."[4] Women's abilities to heal and redirect the community was not a new theme for Neshat, but in the months before and after 9/11 an allegorical female model became more pronounced in her scripts. Still, *Logic of the Birds* is a curious moment in Neshat's career: produced for the localized audience of a small experimental space near the West Village, it deviated from her recently attained International presence

Globality at the Millennium

Apart from film-stills, Neshat moved away from photography after 1997, and by 9/11 she was recognized primarily for video installations with increased demand for her work in international museums and exhibitions following her triumph at the 1999 Venice Biennale. The photographs she produced for *Women of Allah* were, as she described, "minimalist, sculptural, rigid" but were also complex signs relying on a trade of contradictory images and meanings for Iranian women specifically and Muslim women generally. Amna Malik references Douglas Crimp's postulation that Minimalism imbues a theatrical quality to photography and film by "psychologizing pictorial images" that position Neshat's aesthetic transformation from politicized portraits to lyrical video installations. In Malik's view, neither are "easily detected as transgressive but depends on the spectator's cultural familiarity."[5] I have suggested that Neshat's work operates transculturally to achieve a dual transgression, and Minimalism not only refers to sculpture installation, Land Art, and pictorial construction in the West but to the subversive quality of Persian poetry and post-Revolutionary Iranian film. Neshat notes that the formal language of Minimalism in her work services a critique of society "without claiming to do so."[6] Although she addressed repression by the IRI, she was not interested in its specific structure, nor Iran's political history generally, but in a "sense of resistance" that comes from women's actions daily.[7] Neshat eschewed overt politics for a stylized, minimalist rendering of this general "sense," communicating psychological impressions under patriarchy through an "Eastern/Islamic" context that satisfied curatorial calls for difference.

However, an 'axis of evil' within a 'clash of civilizations' suddenly characterized as East/West and Islamic/Christian bolstered post-9/11 political rhetoric against which Okwui Enwezor suggested that artistic responses and centers of culture could counteract the hegemonic fuel to the struggle, even citing then-President Mohammad Khatami's call for renewed dialog. From Islamophobic reactions such as the 2004 law against headscarves in France to further Islamist attacks including railway bombings in London and Madrid, Enwezor asserted that such dialog is best situated by "biennales [as] natural spaces of thought and curatorial experiment capable" of addressing these tensions.[8] He claimed that international mega-exhibitions, often facilitated within developed countries and their metropolises, were not solely presenting an avant-gardism as much as forging a "will to globality." Rather than picturing worlds for audience consumption, he saw their potential "to see in the biennial phenomenon the possibility of a paradigm shift in which we as spectators are able to encounter many experimental cultures without possessing them." As "the space where the problem of cultural translation arises" the international biennial became a discursive site for the signs of mass mobility taking place under globalization, where transnational and transcultural attitudes toward identity, nationality, and citizenship coalesce in "an open-ended relationship with a variety of institutional productions and private experiences."[9]

Enwezor's summations marked a pronounced shift toward the political in biennial culture at the millennium, positioned as a "global scene of cultural translation." Acknowledging that these spaces of cultural production were tied to broader economics, including tourism and revitalization, he still positioned them as diasporic public spheres where global flows of information accumulate in proximity to the West's modes of thought and practice, including epistemological contradictions such as post-colonial theory. Evolving from Guy Debord's *Society of the Spectacle*, Enwezor's strategic globalism coopts the spectacularization of the art experience – its agents, diffusions, and general viewers – as produced through biennial culture, turning it over from its capitalist consumptive model of the spectatorial gaze and toward counter-hegemonic subjectivities and frameworks. In these spaces of spectacle exhibition, knowledge of the world could resist didacticism, destabilized *at the limit* within a third-space of encounters. But such encounters would require new media to carry exhibitions and their institutions into the twenty-first century.

The availability of video had replaced celluloid as artists' filmic media until the reemergence of 16 and 35-mm film. According to Erika Balsom, this return to the analog reavowed cinema among artists as a cultural vernacular of collective memory. It also came to dominate museums and curatorial practice in part due to projection's mobility and affordability. The notion of capital, both economic and cultural, was supplied by the spectacle of moving-image projection and offered a high-brow entertainment for the cosmopolitan traversing global exhibitions and museums of modern/contemporary art. Still, Balsom maintains the earnestness of artists working with cinema as a nostalgic form to "forget the world in order to return to it" and the virtual qualities of moving-images to interrogate "physical reality and its representation."[10] The institution's novelty for new media and the multi-million dollar architecture to house it, or the biennial's reliance upon consumptive spectacle to sustain its networks of local/global economic dependency, provide less spaces of criticality as discursive sites for considering whose-art-for-whom.

Counteracting Enwezor's claims for strategic globalisms that can take full advantage of recent art's spectacle nature to engage with audiences, one should ask who these audiences were? Many terms surface, and Enwezor was partial to the viewer as "cosmopolitan," one who comes to understand others through the metropolitan centers of diaspora that often facilitate spaces of global exhibition. But the cosmopolitan's travel is freely chosen, supported by the financial resources and educational underpinnings necessary to travel to a Venice Biennale or Sao Paulo Biennial. Caroline A. Jones notes in her encyclopedic *The Global Work of Art* that the cosmopolitan "always resides within a specific 'cosmos,' one not necessarily open to all" and, echoing Immanuel Kant, is allied to a Western ideal of knowledge.[11] A salient example, Harald Szeemann, whose itinerary as a curator-auteur arguably began with the 1972 documenta, favored phenomenological and conceptual experiences, easily transportable across borders. His approach, moving away from the exhibition-model of sculpture and painting to the artist-production of environments and processes to be activated, was a defining influence on curation. Jones further accounts that the transnational production of biennial culture – its artists, curators, and visitors – often alienated a local art network in favor of aesthetic value for a global audience. But "internationalism" as a framework of exhibition was long overladen by economics and politics before epistemological concerns.

The (Next) New Internationalism

Internationalism emerged in post-World War I Europe as a new approach to global politics with economic and cultural exchange as a pathway to peace among nations. "New Internationalism" was connected to visual art sometime later, as colonialism was coming to an end and the Cold War was producing its own cultural manipulations. In *Art Since Mid-Century: The New Internationalism*, Werner Haftmann referred to Venice, Kassel, and Sao Paolo as centers where the next artistic language could be investigated. Although this suggests a highly modernist approach to art, determining a scale of influence via nations and style, the exhibition as a spatial/temporal center of dialog provided a prescriptive model for the internationalism of visual art. On the heels of the Cold War and watershed exhibitions like *Magiciens de la Terre*, following postmodernism's assault on metanarratives and the burgeoning fields of counter-normative theory (queer, post-colonial, critical race, etc.), the Institute for International Visual Art was founded and held its first symposium at the Tate Gallery in Spring 1994, *Global Visions: Towards a New Internationalism in the Visual Arts*.

The term's currency grew in part to InIVA founder Gavin Jantjes's 1993 essay *The Long March from 'Ethnic Arts' to 'New Internationalism.'* Although the symposium was originally local in its focus, intending to consider Britain's relationship to globality in art, its essays and presenters – Hal Foster, Judith Wilson, Geeta Kapur among them – heralded a move beyond multiculturalism, to separate itself from the Imperialist discourse of modernity under which terms such as "ethnic" or "primitive" arts emerged and recognize the Euro-American metropolises as new centers for diverse populations to articulate in multiple, challenging ways. Particularly as a curatorial strategy, New Internationalism promised inclusive support of non-white, non-Western artists. However, as Mark Crinson argued, if these strategies were to be successful in challenging long-standing mechanisms of museum and exhibition practices in the West, their most important concept would be translation.[12] Unlike multiculturalism, the exhibition as translatory space would need to produce difference rather than didacticism.

Unfortunately, for all the strides recent exhibitions had made toward inclusivity, they fell short of such translation. The 1993 Whitney Biennial marked changes in curatorial attitudes toward nationhood and its voice(s) but offered no alternative discourses to the victim/oppressor trope of "multiculturalism," an attitudinal approach favoring center/periphery binaries that present minority identity and victimhood in a seemingly inseparable paradigm. In *Magiciens de la Terre*, Jean-Hubert Martin attempted to counteract the modernity of the twentieth-century from which primitive and ethnic arts emerged. Rather than select non-Western artists for diluted modern styles or reductive representations of cultural heritage, Martin's curatorial choices were numerically even across continents in a massive exhibition of 250 artists. But Hubert's plan wasn't without its critics. At the InIVA symposium, Gerardo Mosquera asserted that few international shows are curated at the margins and that the "center" curator created only another level of Imperialism, something to be imported from the "Third World" and reliant on "First World" authority.[13] Another InIVA collaborator, Homi Bhabha defined multiculturalist exhibition practice as a "universalism that permits diversity while also creating ethnocentric norms."[14] They allow diversity, but deny liminality, which is the shared space of difference within Bhabha's third-space between global and local, where there are perpetual forms of translation by which "all cultures are in a process of hybridity." The translatory space in a global framework of cultural exchange became the centralizing idea of art under the concept 'New Internationalism' but its paradigms, including "universality," were determined from the West as the center of economic and curatorial forces.

Internationalism cannot exist separately from politics, traceable as it is to the tensions surrounding the 1937 World's Fair held the same year as Germany's *Entartete Kunst*. In that historical moment, art was intrinsically bound to cultural expressions of national ideologies. Following World War II, cosmopolitanism quickly returned to Europe, although a lingering nationhood with modernist emphasis upon characteristic styles from geographic centers and the colonialist desire for difference remained. A neutralization of mid-century nationalism at the end of the Cold War – and "universalism" as the means to replace it – was embedded in the rhetoric of New Internationalism. Jones defines the primacy of globalism in the 1990s, its move away from the nation-state model of international exchange, as a "tactics of the trans" (translational, transnational, transcultural) under which "internationalism" and the "world picture" of its curation were destabilized: "New terms were needed for new states of being – no longer about relations between nations secured behind borders, but a desiring and restless globality that knits citizens together through nets, nodes, and webs."[15] Complicating that "desiring globality," previous systems of cultural exchange persisted, scrutinized though they were under post-colonial critique at the InIVA Symposium and later at the 1997 conference on biennials organized at Lake Como by the Rockefeller Foundation and Arts International. Further dialog would be made in print, with roundtable discussions (*Artforum*, 2003) and essay-series (*October* 2011), and symposia like *The Idea of the Global Museum* conference at Staatliche Museen, Berlin (2016) that continue debates on the intersections between globality, capitalism, and culture.

Neshat's video installations were tied to specific cultural representations while bearing out complexities of cultural translation in the global present. Her images and imaginings of women in chador provided a visual rhetoric of difference, simultaneously referencing her own longings and rememories from displacement. Demanding an embodied, experiential viewership, she disrupted modes of subject representation to render the encounter afresh. These qualities helped secure her as a leading artist among international circuits, meeting the demands for universality that transnational artists were perhaps best equipped to shape. However, Neshat's work was often addressed according to its binaries – East/West, male/female, private/public, religious/secular – a distillation oversimplifying its complexities and reifying center-periphery models of exchange.

If we understand "global" as spatial and whose borders Enwezor claims are deterritorialized at sites of international exhibition, then the term "universal" should imply an expansion rather than contraction of meaning. But it was imbued with a meta-language of similitude that risks flattening difference. Mosquera addressed Eurocentric "curating cultures" of "curated cultures" as a "neurosis of identity"[16] in which articulations of difference are encoded as exoticism. Non-western artists celebrated by Euro-American curators for their intercultural dialog and "authenticity" would share such criticism. Unlike Hamid Keshmirshekan, who positions exoticism within the ways artists are discoursed, Mosquera placed some responsibility with artists who fulfill these expectations. However, he also noted that resisting curatorial trends is to risk exclusion from economic and exhibition opportunity, advocating a way around by decentralizing curation.[17]

Within models of "curating/curated cultures" is the question of responsibility, whether the supposed exoticism should be borne by the artist or the curator and critics contextualizing their work for audiences. As an example, in 2000 Neshat's *Rapture* was featured at the Bienal de Lyon. A long-awaited follow to his seminal *Magiciens de la Terre,* curator Jean-Hubert Martin settled on *Sharing Exoticisms* as its theme. One review stated that despite the title, nothing about the exhibition was especially exotic; rather, through its thematic organization it expressed a "monolithic hybridization of culture, one that clearly bears the stamp of commodity capital."[18] The exhibition's guiding premise was that international exchange has, indeed, hybridized much contemporary art, and that all cultures are invariably exotic to one another – dismissing the urgent need to investigate flows of information and power along evolving networks of globalization, reassuring "a morally, politically correct stance" in biennial exhibitions and "for the bourgeois elite who mount them."[19]

Jean Fisher, who edited the InIVA panel essays, placed the issue of exoticism with the globetrotting activities of curators that maintain unequal hierarchies of art practices among Europeans and non-Europeans that:

> evade the complex negotiations that must take place between a European aesthetic practice and the rest of the world. For the West to frame and evaluate all cultural productions through its own criteria and stereotypes of otherness is to reduce them to a spectacle of essentialist radical or ethnic typology and to ignore their individual insights…[20]

She goes on to state that non-Euro-American artists comply with their "promotion through commodified signs of ethnicity" or risk exclusion; thereby, they are reduced to an exotic bearer of homogenized signs rather than an individualized and innovative "thinking subject."[21] With theoretical groundwork laid by Bhabha and Stuart Hall, Enwezor's curatorial tactics rejected fixed identity – whether rooted in culture, nation-states, or history – exemplified in work expressed by interdisciplinary practices and informed by cross-cultural experience. Transcending the temporal/spatial conditions of history and the site of international exhibition to regard and understand difference on a level playing field, rather than appease an international meta-language, is the task of universality – one that requires work by curators and critics, artists and viewers.

Pulse, Possessed

Neshat produced three videos in 2001, evermore attenuated to psychological conditions: isolation in *Pulse*, madness in *Possessed*, and death in *Passage*. Each work communicated broadly universal conditions of the human experience from a female perspective within a loosely Middle Eastern context. With this second trilogy, Neshat expressed interest in producing works less reflective of gender inequalities in Iran, further distancing herself from expectations of cultural representation.[22] Significantly, in *Pulse* and *Possessed* an unveiled protagonist emerged, resisting strictly essentialist interpretations. She pared back already-minimal narratives and diminished the viewer's range of vision to a single-screen projection filmed in vibrant color. The new visual style intensified the emotional tenor, resisting strict binary functions that critics and curators adopted to contextualize her work.

Pulse begins with the sound of a pulsating rhythm that fills the gallery. In a single-screen projection of a colorful interior space of deep reds and low light, the camera begins at a distanced high-angle, slowly zooming onto a solitary female figure played by actress Shohreh Aghdashloo. The room's cavernous darkness suggests both privacy and prison. Crouched before a vintage radio, the woman appears to have a melancholy romance with the song that emanates. She sings along softly as the camera produces the vulnerability of her crouched form. The deep space created through the camera's height and slow, steady movement is countered by the rhythmic sound of a pulse. The pulse of a heartbeat, as romantic or life-sustaining, sets an anxious tone to her isolation. The subject is entranced by the radio and its song; the lyrics, sung in duet by Deyhim with Reza Derakhshani, reveal that physical liberation provides an alternative resolution to her longing: "You are all like slaves. When you break loose of the jail of your bodies you are all kings and princes." With words by Rumi and music by Deyhim, the male/female duet recalls that of *Turbulent* but in a private performance. The bodily reference in the Rumi lyrics underpins the eventual close-frame of the woman's form, and the single uninterrupted shot produces a voyeurism and intrusion into a private moment that reveals her intimate communication with the radio-object as a connection to the outside world.

Her next video, *Possessed,* is also a single-screen projection with Aghdashloo as the protagonist. She moves through the alleys of a timeless stone-lined city, compelled by a kind of madness and pressing her body against the walls for guidance and support. The public architecture, linked to the woman's bodily experience of space, is both comforting and imprisoning. Finally, she arrives in a public square, with a look of fear and insanity on her face. The close inspection of Aghdashloo's body and the continuous longshot of her occupied space in *Pulse* calls to mind the cultural surveillance of women's bodies in Iran. The viewer is allowed the scopophilic pleasure of her body, but outside the *andaruni* (private space) the gaze is rebuffed by her maddening stare and gyrations. Her unveiled presence in the public square is an exhibition that eventually causes distress and chaos. *Fetneh* (social chaos) interprets the duality of the plot: first, the woman, driven mad by the rigid social and spatial institutions that contain her, then the people who turn into a mob of confusion. The emergent question is what to do with women, whose repression and resulting rebellion will be at the center of society's collapse? When the protagonist "breaks loose of the jail of her body" it is accomplished by abandoning the veil before reentering the world. Standing atop the public fountain in the square, the people finally begin to take notice and gather around her. Their reactions to the unveiled woman and her behavior vary from supportive to aggressive, mirroring the divided attitudes toward veiling in Iran. The "possessed" woman becomes the metaphor within the crowd's heated debate, at the height of which she slips away unnoticed. As in previous works, the woman achieves liberation through isolation and the transgression of society's boundaries.

Due to the restrictive nature of the IRI toward women, Neshat warns of madness as a potentiality, but thereby freedom as well. Neshat's protagonists reinstate the creative freedom of dissidents, such as Forough Farrokhzad and Sharnush Parsipur, who each questioned the Iranian government under different regimes, provoking accusations of madness to silence and discredit them. Therefore, *fetneh* in *Possessed* may also reference the threat posed by writers, dissidents, and women activists in Iran "where there is no space for individual freedom [and] it becomes very threatening when someone descends into 'madness' and creates chaos."[23] Although Neshat did not initially intend *Possessed* as a sequel to *Pulse*, the co-inclusion of Aghdashloo indicates a structural interest in longer narrative and cinematic form. *Possessed* is the emergence of the protagonist from the "jail of her body" in the isolated room of *Pulse* where she had gone mad. Neshat compares the woman's isolation to the social order, referring to Iran "where one lives under constant social control."[24]

I recognize a pronounced shift in content with Neshat's second trilogy, indicative of her growing wariness with global curation, its demands for translation and cultural representation. Neshat stated that she never wanted to be an "ethnographic artist," only setting out to answer questions about Iran for herself, in personal and philosophical terms.[25] As an Iranian native she has greater insight into the Islamic Republic; but living outside Iran for decades and becoming an American citizen in 1986, she has her own individualized perspective and insights, informed by the trauma of exile and the ongoing development of a hyphenated and hybrid artistic practice. Following her meteoric rise to fame between 1993 and 1999, Neshat had to quickly project ways her work could innovate and offer new possibilities, rather than succumb to rigid categorizations and expectations. In a 2005 interview, she stated that she purposefully sought a "universal language" to move beyond cultural study, stating "All of these topics could be from anywhere; it's just that I present them from my own cultural point of view."[26]

She also confronted the challenge to maintaining her Iranian identity without restricting herself to it:

figuring out how an artist who comes from and remains interested in the resources of another culture can make work that contributes to a broader dialogue... how do you communicate something at a totally international level, without compromising the authenticity of that culture?[27]

As with Neshat, artists described as 'international' interrogated and subverted the representations of socially prescribed identities, in what Mosquera referred to as appropriation, but were seen as pandering to desires for difference rather than negotiating difference "in full knowledge of its seductive alterity, equipping the viewer with the tools for deconstruction" in a Foucauldian "tearing" of the subject.[28] Exchanges between artists and curators who attempted to define a "universal" dialog, consciously separating it from multiculturalism and the Imperialist model of curated cultures, further identified it through experiential works in international exhibition. Neshat's trilogies both determined and were cultivated by demands for multisensory spectacles, which Enwezor optimistically positioned as useful tools for strategic globality. No longer addressed as chiefly negative, co-conspiring with capitalism's affect, spectacle as sited encounters within international exhibition could facilitate "new relations of power and cultural translation."[29]

Cosmopolitan Responsibility/Response-ability

The growing emphasis upon international exhibitions as spaces for exchange rather than consumption, and the centrality of spectacle within it, resulted from a confluence of critical debate and curation. Responding to the 2001

Venice Biennale, Raymond Bellour addressed its large number of moving-image installations as an "other cinema" producing "an aesthetics of confusion" at the new century by which they neither fit comfortably into art or film. Balsom notes, however, that millimeter film as the medium of choice among "video" artists aligned more closely the single authorship traditions of visual artist and director-auteur. Its affordability and image quality aided its preference among both, and as an art of multiples sold in editions of escalating value, fit easily into the market system. Perhaps less obvious, the nature of cinema as communal spectacle replaces "the contemplative temporality of stillness Barthes prized so much in photography." Here, Barthes's specter of the photograph is the flickering specter of the screen, whose transitoriness both captures the passing moment and insists on its irretrievability.[30] Neshat's move from re-presentation in the photograph to embodiment through the moving-image strategically developed a "sensory encounter that invites critical judgment to make sense of the experience."[31] The gaps between stillness and movement, absorption and distanciation, duration of perception and casual contemplation, were collapsing alongside the traditional ways in which objects of visual art and cinema were disseminated and viewed in a renewed cosmopolitanism.

In *Contemporary Art and the Cosmopolitan Imagination* Marsha Meskimmon emphasizes an aesthetic value of cosmopolitanism as something "materially specific and relational" to ethics and the viewing subject. As with Jones's 'tactics of the trans,' the experience-economy produced by curators like Szeemann and their "conditions of transnational, transcultural, and transmedial exchange" provide what Meskimmon views as "aesthetic interventions into the imbrication of place and subject," provoking questions of knowledge, agency, and political commitments in a globalized world. Such profound imbrication cannot occur through the representation of subjects per-se but through the movement of subjects, arguably in a third-space of exchange and through intersubjective practices that "not so much illustrate the subject as materialize subjects-in-process."[32] Meskimmon's model aligns with Jones's trajectory from world's fair to international exhibition, from world-picturing to world-producing. The inherent 'movement' of viewers, the activational forces of multisensory, durational, and affective works of exhibition sprawl are literally spread across host cities requiring days to view. International curators like Enwezor and Bonami sought practitioners, including Neshat, to position encounters as interactive, and moving-images played a particular role in this model of exhibition. Bonami's 2003 Venice Biennale theme, *Dictatorship of the Viewer,* emphasized not only the primacy of the audience in this experience economy but its politicized underpinnings, linking to Enwezor's prediction that the next avant-garde, disregarding any *universal* conception of modernity fused to innovation, would be art as social practice. For *documenta 11* (2002), Enwezor divided his exhibition sprawl across the city of Kassel into 'platforms,' or "forums of committed ethical and intellectual reflection."[33]

Although sometimes criticized as driven by market demands masquerading as ethical engagement, international exhibition can still mobilize viewers in its translatory spaces. However, scrutiny of cosmopolitanism and its identities must be made. Enwezor consistently defines the viewer as the cosmopolitan. Jones also recognizes the cosmopolitan as a traveler who, if the genetics of the World's Fair model remain within Biennials, is challenged to revert to flâneurie rather than critical engagement. Balsom also notes viewer ambivalence in large-scale exhibition, already overwhelmed by a spatial proliferation of works, and the previous chapter addressed how cinema and moving-images dependent upon temporal commitment can either induce or resist casual observation. Terminology like experience-*economy* underscores the very real resources garnered and required in the staging of these exhibitions; put plainly, Biennials necessitate that its visitors have the means to travel freely and purchase entry. These exhibitions are often staged in Europe, but Biennials of the 'Global South' – Sao Paolo, Johannesburg, Havana – also require a robust economic commitment. Both economic and intellectual capital are necessary to these centers and those able to travel for their experience-economies. Jones's "aesthetics of experience," by which she evaluates the production and reception of art in these international contexts, takes into consideration the ways in which *experience* is historically bound to temporary encounters with difference.[34]

As much as international exhibitions invited and sought difference, its contextualizations and ameliorations toward global anxieties offered "universality" as a renewed ethnocentrism translatable to "first-world" audiences. The intellectual spaces of experience, regardless of their claims to counter-hegemony and their insistence upon populism and accessibility, reassert class-bound access and cultural essentialisms. The developed curatorial directives invited diasporic artists both as purveyors of experience and as representatives of an ethnic typology. Demanding more of the viewer than a placating spectacle or sensorial moment requires a politicized framework that for Jones enacts and empowers ethical responses through embodied experiences as the "working of art" (temporal, intellectual, emotional) rather than a work of art. This mode of interaction and its 'workings' Jones further labels as both responsive and responsible, separating the Biennial viewer of the present from the World's Fair flâneur of the past. Within these circuits much globally responsive art produced by diasporic artists is bodily and performative, emphasizing flesh and memory as materially specific, grounded in Maurice Merleu-Ponty's embodied phenomenology. Commencing from there, Meskimmon has devoted much critical attention to the relationship between ethical, responsible viewing within the international exhibition as an embodied, sensory exchange. Individuation of the self occurs through "intercorporeal interdependence" separating viewer from "other(nes)s" and recognizing difference through experiences "embodied and materially located" in spaces opened to the imagination necessary for transformation. Enwezor also credits spaces of exhibition with imagination to deterritorialize futures, and Meskimmon locates the "fully social, fully sensory, subject at the heart of contemporary art's ethical address to the political conditions of globalization" and "the potential to transform social and political life."[35]

In these spaces and potentials Meskimmon frames her 'response-ability,' intersecting Merleau-Ponty and the spatio-temporal exchange of imagination and memory with an aesthetic experience in the present. While she acknowledges that it is impossible to reside in another's flesh, the haptic visuality (as expressed by Laura Marks) compels an empathic engagement of our own bodies and sense memory as an "imaginative extension into the social realm through tactile exchange with embodied others." Response-ability of embodied viewership, as a subjective and phenomenological condition of perception, locks memory/past and imagination/future, dislodging boundaries between self and subject to realize one's socio-political, ethical responsibility toward others. For Meskimmon, "Enabling the links between global politics, ethics, and aesthetics to emerge at the level of the fully social-subject is contemporary art's articulation of a cosmopolitan project."[36] My issue with the strict identification of the subject-viewer as "cosmopolitan," distinct from other identities bound to movement – refugee, diasporic, exilic, migrant – is that it must be resourced by economics and political autonomy necessary to travel freely. But I agree that an embodied experience within the spatio-temporal framework of the international exhibition is best "made operative by artworks that provide access to threshold sensory states" to enable intersubjective connections with others in the world.[37]

Passage

Like her earlier *Rapture*, and similar in theme to *The Logic of the Birds*, *Passage* (Figure 3.1) foregrounds the nomadic and insinuates diaspora. Completing her second trilogy, it was again filmed in Morocco and opens with a line of male mourners carrying a body, lengthening the horizontal expanse of a flat, rocky terrain. Their movement across the desert is slow, making their way along the uneven rocks to the more tractable sand of a beach. Waiting for them is a group of women crouched in a circle. The camera reveals them digging through rock and dry earth in unison, their hands and chadors covered with dirt. The men emerge from somewhere unknown and marked by travel, whereas the women are bound to the earth; engaged in different activities, the men and women are yet unified in purpose. In *Passage*, they are not binary prisoners to their respective public or domestic arenas, nor separated by culture and nature, but joined on the same screen in a shared space and ritual.

The employed camera movements interrelate each work of this trilogy. A slow aerial-zoom of the women reveal a hole they scrape from the desert with their hands. Their rhythmic breath is underscored by chanting that can represent "the labor of birth, the sexual act, or communal ritual."[38] The camera

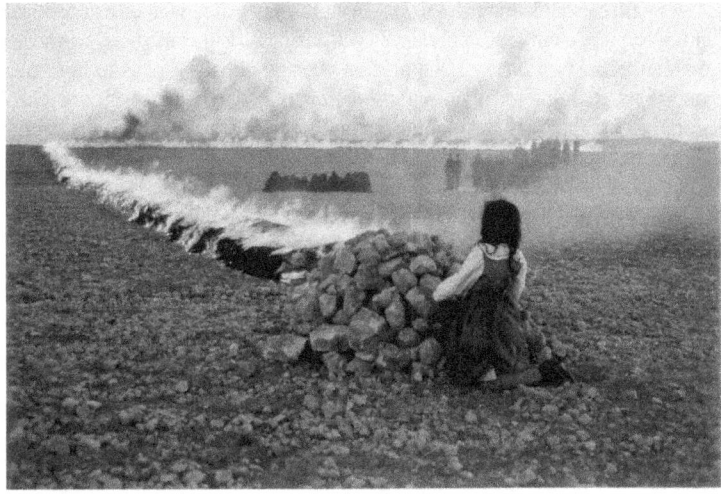

Figure 3.1 Passage, 2001. Film Still (photo by Larry Barns). © Shirin Neshat. Courtesy of the artist and Gladstone Gallery.

zooms out to reveal a little girl playing with rocks; the beginning of life and innocence poised against the seriousness of the adults and death. Although she is engaged in creative mimicry, she is also instructed by what takes place in the world of adults. The little girl building, the women digging, and the men carrying are finally brought together in a single scene. The sun has begun to set, and a stone wall is lit by fire. Darkness and light, beginning and end, life and death are subtle themes from a slow crescendo of multiple actions and mysterious sounds.

In the absence of dual-screen projection, the second trilogy was less engaged with Neshat's "in-between" position and ambiguous narratives were replaced by more tightly woven mis-en-scene. *Passage* also departed from Neshat's process in significant ways, most obviously in the presence of a new composer, Philip Glass. His minimalist composition for *Passage* choreographed the movements of Neshat's actors, whether quick and scattered or slow and determined, but her characteristic elements of breath and chanting within the sound element remained. The concept for *Passage* grew from images of Palestinian funeral processions Neshat had seen on the news, offering the subject matter of death and communal mourning specifically to Glass, who was collaborating on short films with artists such as Atom Egoyan and Michal Rovner. With its rootedness in a Palestinian rite of passage, from life to death, Neshat described *Passage* as her "least Iranian work" to that point, even with chador as one of its central images.[39]

As with Neshat's first trilogy, *Passage* presents veiled women as apolitical and in service to emotive experiences within allegorical constructs. However, less constrained by binaries she paid an ever-pronounced focus to humanist conditions, resisting an ethno-representational language that constrained discourse on her work. In the months leading to 9/11, a frustration, even confusion, within her work was evident in the second trilogy videos. Simultaneous expectations of Iranian-ness and universality, tinged with desire for a politicized viewpoint, further constricted criticality around her work and swayed her to abandon veil-imagery at a time when she was resistant to politics and sensitive to cultural essentialism. Even with the reappearance of chador in *Passage*, the identity of her subjects as Iranian is blurred by the indefinite nature of where they are set, implying that identity and national boundaries are fluid and uncategorizable.

Malik draws on horizontality to tease out "a dialog between the legacy of Minimalism" and "the movement of the body in space." In her account, Minimalism has an inherent relationship to horizontality as an "entry to the space of the everyday from a formalist and phenomenological account in a condition of geography and territory." Here, Minimalism is both artistic practice and metaphoric visual language applied to her discussion of *Rapture* but equally relevant to *Passage* where bodies moving in a vast landscape are openly worlded yet grounded to ritual and everyday human activity. To this I link a Foucauldian turn in Malik's positioning of the "relationship between the sacred and profane, of what constitutes transgression" as highly subjective, opening the need for heterogenous critical strategies "indicative of a fragmentary and dispersed form[s] of knowledge." Transgression as subjective to one's own experience, simultaneously bound and unbound to nation and politics, can be established and shared to "decentralize' knowledge in 'decentered' spaces."[40] The need for 'horizontality,' or 'decentralization,' was first voiced by Mosquera at the InIVA symposium, framing it as a necessary alternative to international exhibition that redistributes curatorial authority to the "curated cultures" and resists token representations of otherness. Artists whose spatial metaphors for globalization and its participatory bodies were often activated through moving-images and installation practices that fasten to Malik's identification of Minimalism's phenomenological legacy.

Participating in this spectatorial and geographical network, Laura Marks asserts intercultural film as "a visible trace of cosmopolitanism," shaped by context and the intercultural audiences it encounters. Thus, the conditions of viewership whether in the international exhibition or the local museum, relationally frame "media arts [that] cannot be conceived of separately from the set of viewers that give them meaning."[41] This relational, intersubjective, and in-time experience is indicative of contemporaneity, under which artists unhinge meaning from strict articulations of history and identity and viewers relinquish any surety of knowledge in the images presented. These translatory conditions destabilize, in Foucauldian terms, identities at the limits of naming and understanding. For Marks, this spatial/temporal suspension is where intercultural film is most transformative, in gaps where artists like Neshat grasp along with the viewer "in search for a language by which to express cultural memory," inevitably recognizing the "inability to speak" or "represent objectively" culture, history, or memory.[42] The silences of subject-protagonists in Neshat's second trilogy, as with her first and the photographs before, are unaccountable to official histories. A strategy of rememory is contingent upon film as material artifact, referencing the past while manifesting a present/future. If vision is embodied and memory is sensorial, then "embodied experience of cinema is important for representing cultural experiences that are unavailable to vision."[43]

Understanding the diasporic or transnational experience requires strategies of engagement that dismantle preconceived identities and official histories, laying the groundwork for a plurality of experiences framed by the same historical moment. Unavailable to vision, Balsom also sees "film as closely linked to disappearance, to the historical trace."[44] Often characterized as "ambiguous," not only because time and place are suspended but linearity and causality are upended, Neshat's work insists upon a subjective, diasporic envisioning of Iran's recent past. Herein lay the limits to naming and understanding, collaboratively transgressed by artist and viewer, and the problem with a cosmopolitan desire for universalism. Engaging Meskimmon's "embodied and materially located" subject, universalist dreams *should* crumble in contemporaneity, yielding a more appropriate subject who must take time to learn from the experience rather than apply interpretive essentialisms. For *documenta 10* (1997), Catherine David claimed that she had resisted both exoticism and universalism in her curatorial endeavor, linking the latter "in the best of cases, to an acceleration of the processes of acculturation and cultural syncretism in the new urban agglomerations, and in the worst, to the demand for market products in the West." Having also co-curated *Passages de L'Image* (1990), the watershed exhibition of moving-image works, David positioned cinematic form similarly to intercultural film – an "alternative sensory media (acoustic, performative, projective)" that contribute 'strategies of emancipation.'[45]

Tooba

Tooba (2002) was Neshat's contribution to Enwezor's turn at *documenta 11* the same year. It begins with a council of men in a dark room chanting repetitively. A crowd of mostly men is in a field, uniformly dressed in black that further compacts them in a mass. They break into a sprint, as if sped on by the chanting, and ending at the square enclosure of a brick wall containing a single tree. Returning to dual-screen projection, these actions are interspersed with the image of a woman, played by the actress Maria de Los Angeles, who is standing cradled within the trunk of the tree. She remains motionless throughout the film with eyes closed. Wearing a simple black sheath, the camera arcs around her face, the lines of age sharing texture with the tree. The left screen reveals the expanse of landscape and rolling hills, and the people line along the wall, peering toward the tree within. Meanwhile, the right screen bears a slow close-up of the woman. Finally, they leap over the wall and the woman disappears into the tree, retreating from their aggression.

Neshat's allegorical interpretation counter-references her previously addressed theme of woman as metaphor for nature, here specifically the mythical character of the woman-tree as sacred.[46] *Tooba* (sacred tree) explores the mythical garden of many cultures including the tree of paradise in the Qur'an and Old Testament. Since adapting Farrokhzad's poems to her early photographs Neshat often makes use of the garden of Persian literature, here imbuing it with significance as a metaphor of freedom and independence knowable through female wisdom. The aggression of the crowd opposes the meditative calmness of the woman in the tree. When she disappears upon their advance, her passiveness is powerful and underestimated, defying the forces that seek to control it. In this sense, the garden of *Tooba* transcends its meaning as spiritual paradise, replacing it with new metaphysical, spatial possibilities most accessible to women. The separation of men and women on opposing screens is replaced by the inside council and the outside people, landscape and enclosure, the many and the one, ending in a garden closed to the aggression and desperation outside.

The separation of the sacred from the political, the desperation of a crowd running from the noise of the officiated council, was precisely the humanist and philosophical response Neshat had long maintained in her work. But in her first major international exhibition after 9/11, audiences were surprised to find no specific social and political realism. Previously, Neshat used Morocco as a surrogate for Iran; now the neutrality of Mexico and its plains of dry grass picture a landscape that could be anywhere, a new intercultural meaning sited in the film's location. Shot outside Oaxaca, the framing of the woman at the center of the tree connects to worship of the Lady of Guadalupe wrapped in a mandorla from Mexican-Catholic tradition. For Western audiences, *Tooba*'s deemphasis of the veil's iconography was an absence of the political, when there was an expectation that Neshat should provide a "platform for dialogue about Muslims."[47] As with *Passage*, *Tooba* received mixed reviews for seeming to dodge the political at a moment of crisis, rejected for the universalism she had been hitherto praised. Individuals are not nation-state ideologies, and official history is something people witness and process personally; art reflects that subjectivity, and Neshat's response is a version of history informed through discursive layers of witnessing and responding to political crises, through diasporic flows and America's mediated interpretations.

In 2003, *Tooba* became Neshat's first work to be exhibited in Tehran at the Museum of Contemporary Art. The woman's perfect placement in the tree obfuscates the absence of hijab and her visible hair, and her disappearance into the tree would be recognizable to similar metamorphoses tales and metaphors of the garden in Persian literature. A liberal government during the reform period of President Khatami was also timely to its exhibition and, apart from *Passage*, *Tooba* was less controversial for an Iranian exhibition context than her photographs or earlier video installations. The essentialized symbolism of the female subject connected easily to the sacred meaning of the tree, while the council of men juxtaposed against the desperate mob who seek refuge in the sacred garden alludes to psychological conditions of fear and anxiety, rather than any specific ideological criticism.

Neshat's work is certainly characterized by its syncretism and experiential viewership. However, her work revealed flaws in the formulation of international exhibitions that deploy signs of difference toward an assertion of universal conditions. Jantjes spoke of Internationalism in the 1990s, its "hybridity and syncretic formations as the confusing moment after Babel."[48] The "new internationalism" became the "new exclusionism" as curator-auteurs became the gatekeepers of an aesthetic meta-language and artists secured their place in prominent galleries *after* appearing within the biennial system, mining artists who tended to be a transnational, nomadic, and diasporic. Still, Enwezor's *documenta* claimed the refusal of colonialist demands upon authentic representation, insisting instead that its prevailing language was moored to transnational form and sensory media. As with Neshat's entry, reception for Enwezor's *documenta* was mixed. Within the year before the exhibition, he presented lectures in New York and Berlin on transnational forms of art where he bore out his hopes for a "strategic globality" that would allow both artistic autonomy from "market, media, and ideological forces" and "new relations of spectatorship whose program of political expression and cultural specificity reworks the notion of spectacle and constructs it as the site of new relations of power and cultural translation."[49] These transnational forms he also expressed as antinomies, adhering them as differentiated as the knowledge and subjectivities of their artists and viewers. Made within diaspora, transnational forms emerge through a perspective once-removed or through a duality that Malik recognizes as a strength of the producing artist, distanced enough to see a culture clearly yet knowledgeable of its artistic practices and modes of communication.[50] Strategies of destabilization in the spectacles of global exhibition, their unsettled floes of travelers between cultures, similarly allow the intellectual distance to participate in transformations of knowledge.

But the tensions of impending war, Islamophobic, Islamist terrorism, and an overdue awareness of American interruption of Iranian democracy stymied such transformational aspirations and fastened ever-tightly essentialisms with regard to expectations of the artist. As recently as 2023, Aruna D'Souza characterized Neshat as the "spokesperson for the cause of Iranian women for her whole career" and in October 2001, Amei Wallach wrote "Neshat's iconic exploration of the heart, mind, and psyche of Islam is increasingly analogous in its visceral intelligence to Frida Kahlo's encapsulation of her own culture."[51] Both statements not only overgeneralize and oversimplify Neshat's work but inscribe her to a role she never claimed. To the latter, Chin-Tao Wu responded in *Third Text* that, "such ghettoized, if not racist, criticism is deeply ingrained in Western Eurocentric discourse."[52] Valentina Vitali similarly assessed that "Interviews, articles, catalogues, and any such material that has been instrumental in creating and promoting 'Shirin Neshat' as a commodity has tended to assess the work's value in terms of notions of ethnicity."[53] In a 2005 interview, Neshat recalled that critics "want to keep the conversation around Iran or Islam ...and think that I am a speaker for that part of the world. A lot of this work is not even about society or global politics. It is about me."[54]

Soliloquy, and the Melancholy of Post-Colonial Nostalgia

Neshat's success both benefited from and was stymied by two trends in contemporary criticism at the turn of the century: first, the consensus that museum contextualization of non-Western art disseminated a flattened understanding of cultures, rooted in homogenizing curation and to which responsive/responsible artists created works described as identity or international art; second, that increased globalization within the art market, international exhibitions, and art fairs also forced these networks to heed diversity. Embodied practices and technological mediations further problematized museology, where collections and sites were interrupted, even if temporarily. Artists whose works reflected these trends were often displayed within an ethno-political contextualization, and Neshat had grown weary of the limitations and expectations of the contemporary art world. To underscore that the first decade of her work was not as interested in politics as much as surrounded by it, attention should be given to the video-installation she made between the trilogies, and between two centuries, as her most auto-biographical piece.

Rather than the philosophical questions emerging from gendered spaces, *Soliloquy* (1999) (Figure 3.2) is thematic to travel and its effects on identity. It is also the last feature of Neshat in chador as the work's protagonist. The viewer stands between dual-projections of Neshat in a choreographed communication with herself in two cityscapes. From a Middle Eastern, ancient city she looks to the opposite screen of the presumably Western, modern city and vice versa, each environment trades equally on alienating the subject. On one screen she looks with sadness to the opposite, back-and-forth longing for here versus there, a complexity of the Iranian diasporic experience of which Neshat has expressed the confusion of desire for home but feeling like an outsider when she returned.[55] As she stands in a busy transit station on one screen, she looks toward the Turkish courtyard with children playing on the opposite. *Soliloquy* is carefully choreographed so that in each location the interior elements of space, such as windows, become mirror images,

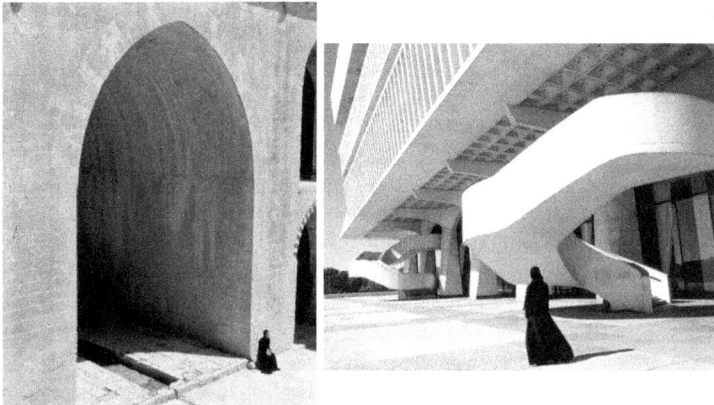

Figure 3.2 (a, b) *Soliloquy,* 1999. Film Stills. © Shirin Neshat. Courtesy of the artist and Gladstone Gallery.

and when the subject looks out onto either a Western or Eastern vista, the revealed structures appear equally iconic: a minaret, for example, opposes a skyscraper. Looking back and forth between the two projections, the viewer is exposed to the separate psychic worlds that are her past and present, her modern life in New York and her Muslim background in Iran. The camera also pans slowly across locations, rendering both temporal and spatial logics depicting each culture in an equal field of vision, revealing both as mysterious, beautiful, and oppressive.

Soliloquy was shot in three cities: Albany, New York, and Mardin, a Kurdish desert-town in Turkey near the borders of Syria and Iran. The Mardin location set a late medieval *Madrasa* (mosque-school) with great stone walls and central courtyard for an architecture generically read as Islamic. In New York, Neshat used the former World Trade Center for its association with modernity and Western capitalism, specifically its entrance to the PATH trains at the base of the building where long disorienting escalators carried thousands of passengers to and from below ground. The handheld camera follows her in chador through the vast crowds, imbricating viewers to her spatial experience. On the opposite screen where she watches children play in the sunlit courtyard, she seems to escape the hurried traffic of bodies in the modern city. Additional exterior shots of the Brutalist architecture of Empire State Plaza in Albany provide a different courtyard, more expansive and with several large, concrete buildings that speak authority through their architecture.

While filming in Mardin, Neshat and her crew discovered that Iranian soldiers were training both Kurdish rebels and Islamic extremists nearby. This dangerous atmosphere led Turkish authorities to tighten security and her crew were under armed guard during the entire production.[56]

Following the 1993 terrorist attack on the WTC, the figure of a woman in chador within the PATH trains station may have elicited a disconcerting image depending on the perspective of the viewer. Thus, art mirrors and foreshadows the uncontrollable co-realities of Islamism and Islamophobic. Under these conditions, it is impossible not to analyze the images in binary constructions. In one projection the dominant architectural landscape is religious and in the other governmental. But when the protagonist wanders from the overwhelming Empire Plaza into one of its buildings, she enters the space of a chapel (filmed in St. Anna's Church, Manhattan) implying that religion is a force also found within those foreboding and authoritative walls. Meanwhile on the opposite screen, she moves from the courtyard to the interior of the Madrasa. Standing on the opposite side of an iron gate, she peers onto what is a vague ritual taking place, related to a funeral by the processional movement of the people. Simultaneously on the opposite screen, the chapel also holds a vague ritual that could be baptism, the people participating look like nuns and monks in gray habits. Within both these projected moments, she watches what is taking place only as an observer; isolated from the action, she leaves into the desert and into the city, respectively. The observational premise emphasizes her exclusion from either location or its activities.

The single interruption of Neshat's dichotomous spaces is the black-and-white projection of a boy lying in the desert. Neshat explains this occasional cut to the boy as a conceptual device to underscore his death.[57] The scene in the old courtyard, where men and women dressed in black arrive from all sides of the building to interrupt the children's play and engage in a funerary ritual, is set against the baptism in the modern chapel. There is past/present, death/rebirth, the end of one geographic existence and its beginning in another, but additionally auto-biographical is a reference to Neshat's recently deceased nephew. *Soliloquy* engages the reality of exilic life, in which participation in even a family funeral is rendered difficult or impossible. The ambiguity of the funerary process, the child left unburied and lying in a desert, pairs that irresolution of mourning.

The emphasis on travel and movement is symbolic of liminality for diasporic subjects. More than any of Neshat's works, *Soliloquy* continually subordinates the subject to a paternalist architecture, moving against and through its thresholds, indicative of Neshat's deeply personal and intellectual understanding of self and environment since those lost paintings she made as a young student. Aerial and long shots of Neshat's tiny form against these architectonic backdrops exaggerate the overwhelm, instilling a dislocational anxiety and psychological exile to both geographies. In concrete or stone, the heaviness of these paternalized spaces express a similitude of authority against which the veiled figure determinedly moves through, and which are projectionally mirrored at key points, a doubling of patriarchy that also affords her a new imaginary space. Expressing the mirror as a utopia,

Foucault positions sites as psychological, beyond the actual and geographical, inverted and transcended.

> In the mirror, I see myself where I am not, in an unreal, virtual space that opens behind the surface; I am over there, there where I am not, a sort of shadow that gives me visibility to myself, that enables me to see myself there where I am absent...[58]

Far from a narrative solely of nostalgia and loss, *Soliloquy* emblematizes spatial ambivalence and allegorizes the female figure as perpetually in movement against her borders. To this experience both spaces dissolve into the rhetoric of her imagination and transformation, and at the video's end Neshat drenches herself with cleansing water.

Narratives of displacement often focus on loss – of culture, language, and community – but Marks notes that "loss alone cannot explain the transformations and productions of culture that occur in diaspora."[59] Neshat operates within the networks, channels of information, and modes of practice of her host country while in collaboration with artists from her home. Her displaced status as a young, lonely student who could barely speak English cannot be understated, and her position as a transnational artist in New York grants her the ability to safely address political and gendered conditions in Iran while transgressing fixed identities. After her 1995 interrogation, Neshat most often referred to herself as an exile, predicating her subject matter on individual experience more than a diasporic, communal one. Originally from a culture that emphasizes collectivity, this approach more deeply embeds her creative framework within Western Enlightenment concepts and artistic practices of the body, often portraying individuals as isolated but powerful. New knowledge becomes possible as people move between cultures, against which identities reshape and transgress the limits of nostalgia.

Foucault's "aesthetics of existence" rely on practices of self-production and emphasize instability over fixity in order to recognize lived experience as a constant performativity. Likewise, cultures and the gender relations they produce are ever in flux. From the Greek, nostó (I return) and alghó (I feel pain), nostalgia need not weaponize, immobilize, or cling to the past but must strategize "the ability of past experience to transform the present."[60] As a living being in this world, Fisher's "thinking subject," Neshat cannot help but respond and create women who, as with herself, must be outcast or self-exiled. Troubling the false securities of naming and identifying while recognizing her own nostalgia for Iran and its traumatic loss was the paradox of Neshat's first decade of work, auratic expressions of the tempo-spatial dislocations of the subject. Dispelling exoticism and idealism of her exilic condition, she admits that she would have been unable to produce her work in Iran or without that transnational perspective.[61] Using this perspective to her advantage, her work continues to remind us that identity and culture can never entirely be represented from a single vantage point. By virtue of the discourse that *surrounds* them, Neshat's veiled bodies represented a politicization of gender, but particularly female viewers would be hard-pressed not to recognize their psychologies, further imbricating the embodied experience of her video installations. The contested female body reminds us that women across the world are ineradicably positioned by their gender – culturally, socially, and economically. While this realization is fortified as a dialog of the "universal," geopolitical realities should be recognized via an engagement with difference as a function of ethically responsible viewership.

Notes

1 Wallach, Amei. "Theatre: An Islamic Culture in All Its Beauty." *The New York Times* (Sept. 30, 2001) Sunday Ed, p. 6. Wallach's article about the production and pending debut of Logic of the Birds came to include a recounting of Neshat's personal experience of 9/11.
2 Ebrahimian, Babak. "Passage to Iran: Shirin Neshat Interviewed." *PAJ: A Journal of Performance & Art*, vol. 24, no. 3 (Sept. 2002). p. 51.
3 Wallach, Amei. "Theatre: An Islamic Culture in All Its Beauty."
4 Brisebois, Marcelle and Paulette Gagnon. *Shirin Neshat*. Castello di Rivoli Museo de Arte (2002). p. 168.
5 Malik, Amna. "Surface Tension: Reconsidering Horizontality in the Work of Diasporic Iranian Artists." Harris, Jonathan ed. *Identity Theft: The Cultural Colonization of Contemporary Art*. Liverpool: Liverpool University Press, 2008. 109–134. p. 112.
6 Ibid.
7 Naghibi, Nima. *Rethinking Global Sisterhood: Western Feminism & Iran*. Minneapolis: University of Minnesota Press, 2007. p. 53.
8 Enwezor, Okwui. "The Politics of Spectacle: The Gwangju Biennale and the Asian Century." *7th Annual Gwangju Biennale, Exhibition Catalog* (2008), 12–39. p. 18.
9 Enwezor, Okwui. "Mega-Exhibitions and the Antinomies of a Transnational Global Form." *Documents*, vol. 23 (Spring 2004), 426–445. p. 440.
10 Balsom, Erika. *Exhibiting Cinema in Contemporary Art*. Amsterdam: Amsterdam University Press, 2013. p. 181–182.
11 Jones, Caroline A. *The Global Work of Art*. Chicago: Chicago University Press, 2016. p. 169.
12 Crinson, Mark. "'Fragments of Collapsing Space': Postcolonial Theory and Contemporary Art." Jones, Amelia ed. *Companion to Contemporary Art Since 1945*. Oxford: Blackwell Publishing, 2006. p. 464.
13 Mosquera, Gerardo. "Some Problems in Transcultural Curating." Fisher, Jean ed. *Global Visions: Towards a New Internationalism in the Visual Arts*. London: Kala Press & The Institute of International Visual Arts, 1994. p. 136.
14 Bhabha, Homi. "The Third Space." Rutherford, Jonathan ed. *Identity: Community, Culture, & Difference*. London: Lawrence & Wishat, 1990. p. 210.
15 Jones, Caroline A. *The Global Work of Art*. p. 152.
16 Mosquera, Gerardo. "Some Problems in Transcultural Curating." p. 136.
17 Mosquera, Gerardo. "The Marco Polo Syndrome: Some Problems around Art and Eurocentrism," *Third Text*, vol. 21 (Winter 1992/93): 35–41.
18 Kaufman, Jason Edward. "Grasping the Global." Artnet (online), 2000.
19 Ibid.
20 Fisher, Jean. "The Syncretic Turn: Cross-Cultural Practices in the Age of Multiculturalism," in *Theory in Contemporary Art Since 1985* ed. Zoya Kocur and Simon

Leung (Oxford 2005); quoted in Hamid Keshmirshekan, "The Question of Identity vis-à-vis Exoticism in Contemporary Iranian Art," *Iranian Studies*, 43, no. 4 (Sept. 2010), 501.
21 Ibid.
22 MacDonald, Scott. "Between Two Worlds: An Interview With Shirin Neshat." *Feminist Studies*, vol. 30, no. 3 (Fall 2004). p. 648.
23 Naficy, Hamid. "Veiled Vision/Powerful Presences: Women in Post-revolutionary Iranian Cinema." Afkhami, Mahnaz & Erika Friedl ed. *In the Eye of the Storm: Women in Post-Revolutionary Iran.* Syracuse, NY: Syracuse University Press, 1994. p. 141.
24 Ibid., p. 142
25 Camhi, Leslie. "Lifting the Veil." *ArtNews* vol. 99, no. 2 (Feb. 2000), 148–151. p. 151.
26 Brisebois, Marcelle and Paulette Gagnon. *Shirin Neshat*. Montreal: Musee d'art contemporain de Montreal, 2001. p. 119.
27 Ebrahimian, Babak. "Passage to Iran: Shirin Neshat Interviewed," p. 48.
28 Jones, Caroline A. *The Global Work of Art*. p. 229.
29 Enwezor, Okwui. "The Black Box." *Documenta 11_Platform 5: Exhibition Catalogue.* Stuttgart: Hatje Cantz, 2002. p. 42–55. (43–44)
30 Balsom, Erika. *Exhibiting Cinema in Contemporary Art*, p. 79–80.
31 Jones, Caroline A. *The Global Work of Art*. p. 198.
32 Meskimmon, Marsha. *Contemporary Art and the Cosmopolitan Imagination.* New York: Routledge Press, 2011. p. 6.
33 Enwezor, Okwui. "The Black Box," p. 43.
34 Jones, Caroline A. *The Global Work of Art*. p. 201.
35 Meskimmon, Marsha. "Making Worlds, Making Subjects: Contemporary Art and the Affective Dimension of Global Ethics." *World Art*, 1:2, 2011. 189–196. p.191–192.
36 Meskimmon, Marsha. *Contemporary Art and the Cosmopolitan Imagination.* p.35–40.
37 Ibid.
38 Brisebois, Marcelle and Paulette Gagnon. *Shirin Neshat*. p. 120.
39 Ravenal, John B. "Shirin Neshat: Double Vision." Broude, Norma and Mary D. Garrard eds. *Feminist Art History After Postmodernism*. Berkeley: University of California Press, 2005. p. 450.
40 Malik, Amna. "Surface Tension: Reconsidering Horizontality in the Work of Diasporic Iranian Artists." p. 130.
41 Marks, Laura U. *The Skin of the Film: Intercultural Cinema, Embodiment, and the Senses*. Durham: Duke University, 2000. p. 19.
42 Ibid., p. 21.
43 Ibid., p. 22.
44 Balsom, Erika. *Exhibiting Cinema in Contemporary Art*, p. 101.
45 Jones, Caroline A. *The Global Work of Art*. p. 229.
46 Khazini, Dorna. "Shirin Neshat." *The Believer* (Aug., 2003). p. 100.
47 Azari, Shoja & Shirin Nehsat. "In Movement: A Conversation With Shirin Neshat." *Shirin Neshat, 2002–2005*. New York: Charta & Barbara Gladstone Gallery, 2005. p. 8.
48 Jantjes, Gavin. "The Long March from 'Ethnic Arts' to 'New Internationalism.'" Lavrijsen, Ria ed. *Cultural Diversity in the Arts: Art, Art Policies, & the Facelift of Europe*. Amsterdam: Royal Tropical Institute, 1993. 59–66.
49 Enwezor, Okwui. "Mega-Exhibitions and the Antinomies of a Transnational Global Form," p. 444.
50 Malik, Amna. "Surface Tension: Reconsidering Horizontality in the Work of Diasporic Iranian Artists," p. 110.

51 D'Souza, Aruna. "Shirin Neshat." *Four Columns* (February 17, 2023) and Wallach, Amei. "Theatre: An Islamic Culture in All Its Beauty."
52 Wu, Chin-Tao. "Worlds Apart: Problems of Interpreting Globalised Art." *Third Text*, vol. 21, no. 6 (Nov. 2007), 719–731. p. 724.
53 Vitali, Valentin. "Corporate Art and Critical Theory: On Shirin Neshat." *Women, A Cultural Review*, vol. 15, no. 1 (March 2004), 1–18.
54 Wu, Chin-Tao. "Worlds Apart: Problems of Interpreting Globalised Art," p.724.
55 Vitali, Valentin. "Between Art and Culture: A Conversation with Shirin Neshat." *n.paradoxa*, vol. 12. p. 33–43.
56 MacDonald, Scott. "Between Two Worlds: An Interview With Shirin Neshat," p. 640.
57 Ibid., p. 641.
58 Foucault, Michel. "Of Other Spaces." *Diacritics*, vol. 16 (Spring 1986), 22–27. p. 25.
59 Marks, Laura U. *The Skin of the Film: Intercultural Cinema, Embodiment, and the Senses*, p. 195.
60 Ibid., p. 201.
61 Heartney, Eleanor. "Shirin Neshat: Living Between Cultures." Heartney, Eleanor, Helaine Posner, Nancy Princenthal, and Sue Scott eds. *After the Revolution: Women Who Transformed Contemporary Art*. New York: Prestel, 2007, p. 230–251.

4   From Transgression to Aesthetic-Political Commitment

Neshat's Iran at the Crossroads

In 1995, Neshat was detained and interrogated at the Tehran airport, which she described as one of the most terrifying experiences of her life.

> A few hours seemed like a lifetime. I sat there in the presence of this bearded man, watching him open and close file cabinets, looking through folders, occasionally glancing at me with disgust.[1]

The encounter with Iranian authorities was profoundly traumatic, and to date she has not returned to Iran. She later considered filming *Tooba* in her family's former farm near Qazvin, and there was discussion with her brother to secure a visa; but history once again intervened, and travel to-and-from Iran became inconceivable with 9/11. After *Tooba's* reception at documenta and her hopes of visiting Iran deferred, Neshat expressed that she was finished with an art world that often misinterpreted her work. She began to focus on producing a film with broader appeal beyond art world audiences.[2]

With its more conventional narrative structure and less ambiguity, *The Last Word* (2003) was Neshat's most dramatic leap toward cinema. Based on writer Sharnush Parsipur's censorship and incarcerations, the 18-minute piece arguably relates Neshat's own terrifying interrogation as well. *The Last Word* is an imaginary return, exorcising her traumatic experience and tributing the many creative individuals and activists who have been surveilled, harassed, and imprisoned. Through making *The Last Word*, Neshat became more interested in the work of Parsipur, whose novel *Women Without Men* was published in Iran in 1989 and subsequently banned. Parsipur was imprisoned for more than four years, in part for the politics of her brother, and survived three additional incarcerations of months-long terms. One sentence was against her open discussion of virginity in *Women Without Men*, and the Ministry of Islamic Culture and Guidance eventually desisted her authorship. Her publisher was shut down and she finally exiled to New York in 1994.

An elderly woman in a blue shroud leads an unveiled female protagonist down a dark passage and into a room. Separated by a long table, she is seated across from a bearded man shuffling through a large book. His side is the

DOI: 10.4324/9781003341192-5

bureaucratic order of power, books scattered across the table as evidence of the many people who have been threatened under its authority. Shrouded in darkness, the woman sits on the side of imagination and memory. Men are cast in varying degrees of light and shadow behind him, looking through an array of books and file cabinets in a warehouse setting. At first, the interrogator tries to ameliorate her discomfort, then annoyed by her silence he intimidates and threatens. Stating in Persian, "You keep your distance, but we keep our eye on you" suggests the constant threat artists may face in Iran, often forcing them into exile. The vision of a little girl appears at the end of the table, and the woman finally responds to his queries in a poetic language: "…. when my life was no longer anything nothing but the tick-tock of a wall clock, I discovered that I must … must love madly, one window is enough for me, one window of consciousness, looking and silence…."[3]

As the woman recites the poem to her interrogator, its lines appear across the bottom of the screen in translation. Neshat's only video to that date to incorporate subtitles, the communication of an intentional message clearly emblematized the work as political. Returning to the poetry of Forough Farrokhzad, *The Window* is recited in its entirety; like the male figure in *Turbulent*, the interrogator appears awestruck by the beauty, creativity, and strength of the woman's achievement through her verse. As with *Rapture,* the woman's courage and actions liberate her while the men shuffle meaninglessly through their books. Referencing her earlier works, Neshat inserts her own artistic contributions within the legacy of imprisoned and censored Iranian writers with whom she identifies. Allegories of wisdom and innocence lie in the enigmatic figures: the old woman, seen standing behind the poet at intervals of her interrogation, and the little girl who leads her from the room.

According to Eleanor Heartney, the reappearance of poetry at various intervals in Neshat's work signifies its importance to her "as a symbol of eroticism and mystery which no social or religious order can erase."[4] Farrokhzad's poem addressed a totalitarian regime, in her case during the second Pahlavi era. Seven years after her own interrogation in Tehran Neshat was perhaps secure enough under the reform government to explore the galvanizing event that resulted in her exile, but she was just as likely influenced by the post-9/11 period of interrogation of Muslim citizens and deeply debated concerns over civil liberties.

I am in a strange position that reached its peak after September 11. I am a New York citizen. I watched this evidence, and I cannot possibly support whoever was responsible. But am I going to go join the bandwagon of saying "Oh yes, all these barbaric Moslems? … I have to say that there is so much injustice across the board that you have to look at the political history. And here I am not just talking about Iran but the Moslem world… And yet I am American, I am Iranian, but I'm just an artist. The most I can do is show how complicated everything is.[5]

Although embedded in a transnational perspective, her address of "political history" and its complexities suggests transition, from philosophical response to an aesthetic-political commitment, and then from the art-world audience of international exhibition to popular viewership with cinema. *The Last Word* departed from her choreographed dual-screen placement, deemphasizing binary readings to an individual testimony, politicizing the piece despite its allegorical signs.

From the same interview, Neshat emphatically asserted: "I am not an activist. I am not a feminist. I am an artist from Iran, living here." Neshat aligned the irresponsibility of speaking on behalf of Iranian/Muslim women at odds with activism, and her concurrent viewpoint on feminism evidenced an irresolution with its differentiated practices in the West and Iran.[6] However, *The Last Word* titularly thematizes the seizure of authority by the woman's poetic defiance, positioning a slippage in Neshat's self-identifications in relationship to her practice. Socio-political interpretations were embedded in the discourse and criticality on her work since its inception. But an aesthetic-political practice is best understood through processes of translation and horizontality rather than a privileged, cosmopolitan universality, and best articulated in filmic strategies that attenuate embodied experience. A pronounced shift occurred in Neshat's work precisely ten years after its debut, at which she arrests its socio-political criticality and asserts her own aesthetic-political commitment with an appropriate cinematic style of the investigative gaze, which Laura Mulvey positions as endemic to feminist film as transgressive media.

Women Without Men

Laura Marks's groundbreaking research places intercultural film as a genre produced in Euro-American metropolises, representative of living between two or more cultural regimes of knowledge and expressive of a diasporic experience embodied beyond the visual. Mulvey's recent investigations of women's film also bear out the interrelationship of the corporeal and transgression into a particular cinematic style that fuses the materiality of the body with that of the film, challenging the distance between spectator and viewer. In conversation with Martine Beugnet, they reassessed the psychoanalytic discourse of feminist film (that Mulvey herself was instrumental in establishing), forging a path between the psychological and experimental into a "form of embodied thought" that "moves us both viscerally and intellectually."[7] These theories of film readily apply to Neshat's first feature, its techniques of cinematography, sound, framing, symbolism, narrative device, and the corporeality of its female characters elicit affective confusion in what can alternatively be labeled "corporeal cinema" or "cinema of transgression."

In January of 2003, Neshat attended a Writer's Workshop Lab at the Sundance Film Institute to explore scriptwriting for feature-length films.

From the experience, she first made *The Last Word* before adapting Parsipur's *Women Without Men.* The novel is primarily set in a home outside Tehran with a mystical garden and orchard, where five women have come to convene in refuge from their traumas and unhappiness, a thematic escape Neshat recently explored in *Tooba* and *The Logic of the Birds.* With Shoja Azari, credited for the first time as her directorial collaborator, she brought a diverse film crew of mostly diasporic Iranians and Europeans to Morocco for the five-year project. In that time, the film was also dissected into separate video installations for each character: *Mahdokht* (2004), *Zarin* (2006), *Munis* (2008), *Faezeh* (2008), and *Farokh Lega* (2008). These formats, from video installation to film, evidence the transmutable quality of her work across exhibition and cinematic contexts, as well as the fluidity of contemporary art's moving-images, transiting between museums and cinemas, galleries and film festivals.

Parsipur's novel is split into five parts narrating the stories and perspectives of each character, further divided between Tehran and a rural orchard in the 1950s. This blueprint of plot, character, and site offered a structural simplicity for Neshat and Azari to navigate, although the book's magic-realist style afforded a challenging translation. Parispur communicates, through a balance of fantastical elements set against historical events, the misogynies of Iranian society and its psychological effects on five women from its different strata. Munis and Faezeh are middle-class friends who are past their marriageable prime. Faezeh is traditional and desires to marry Munis's religiously conservative brother, whereas Munis is far more interested in the country's current political crisis than being coerced into marriage. Farokh Lega, renamed Fakhri in the film, is an affluent middle-aged woman who leaves an uncaring husband and purchases the orchard as her personal retreat. With her wisdom and wealth, she seems the most empowered but is also beleaguered by ageism and its limitations. Zarin is lowest in the social hierarchy; a prostitute who no longer speaks and is hallucinating every man she encounters as faceless. She occupies some of the most powerful scenes in the film: incessantly scrubbing her body raw in a bathhouse and levitating above a pond in the garden. Whether in a debasing brothel or healing garden she is the most vulnerable to her surroundings, and closely represents Iran/Islam's most marginalized female figure.

Apart from Mahdokht, each of the characters is living in Tehran before escaping to the orchard. Mahdokht is a woman who wants many children, but is deeply uncomfortable with sex, exacerbated by cultural and religious attitudes. Mahdokht's thoughts reveal a preoccupation with the fate of the country's orphans while clinging to her virginity which is "like a tree." As an alternative to sex, she plants herself in the orchard so that she will bear fruit and spread seeds. Neshat interprets Mahdokht's obsession and fear as a descent into madness; grounded into the earth, she obsessively knits miles of yellow yarn. In a vibrantly memorable image, a legion of children in bright yellow sweaters run in a forested backdrop on two screens while Mahdokt emerges from a misty pond and manically knits on a third screen between. The themes of woman-as-tree and a magical garden space recur from Neshat's previous work, as well as a madness that allows the woman to forge a path toward liberation. Neshat's *Mahdokht* occupied a complete fantasy that matches the character's stream-of-conscious thoughts in the novel. In her oeuvre, it remains a unique, standalone installation – her only three-channel – and its absence from the final feature allowed more screentime for the historical events against which Parsipur's novel is set.

Excluding the fantastical story of *Mahdokht* from the final film, Neshat restructured the plot toward tighter narrative coherence.[8] She developed Munis's story to include intentional engagement with the historical events of August 1953. Parsipur merely mentions the time frame, its temporal allusion used to exemplify the women's ability to transcend history's episodes. The specific circumstances and consequences of the coup-d'etat of Prime Minister Mohammad Mosaddegh is reduced to a vague description of violence in the streets. In contrast, Neshat emphasizes the coup staged by British forces with the assistance of the newly formed Central Intelligence Agency (CIA) of the U.S. Factual details play over radios, overshadowing the women's lives, particularly Munis. In a scene reminiscent of Neshat's 2001 video *Pulse*, she crouches before the radio in her living room; she wants to be a part of the action but her brother, Amir, forbids her from going outside. Neshat centralizes the intricate ways in which Iranian politics are connected to the lives and minds of women, and therefore the film begins with Munis's suicide.

Munis already appears to transcend earthly existence as she stands in chador over an undulating line of grayish rooftops against brilliant blue sky. It's a minimalist approach to scenography and use of architecture to construct space that is signature of Neshat's style. Peering from the rooftop of her home, Munis sees a political activist lying below, dying from knife wounds. Her desire to leave her earthly limitations and join him is so strong that she leaps from the roof to her death. Munis's dramatic, slow-motion leap from the rooftop appears like floating to the sounds of *Adhaan* (public call to prayer) in the background, but we never see her body impact the pavement. As her chador lifts into the sky, her thoughts are poetic, signaling her death as liberating: "my memory is punctured." In the novel, she returns after a month and her brother, angry at her disobedience and ashamed of her behavior, stabs her; but Neshat refused to include brutal violence against women in the film, turning focus instead to the defiant acts that liberate them.[9]

Faezeh assists Amir with burying Munis in the garden of their home, concealing the shame of her suicide. When Munis calls to Faezeh from beneath the earth to unbury her, Munis's first ghostly action is to enter the male-space of a coffeehouse where she can receive news about the protests. Faezeh follows her and, not daring to go in, garners the attention of two men as she waits outside. Later, Munis finds her crying in a darkened alley, and viewers can assume that she has been raped; again Neshat chose to omit this violence.

Defying reason, Munis somehow knows to lead Faezeh to the orchard (in the book, Karaj, a town northwest of Tehran) where along with Fakhri and Zarin she can heal. In the novel, Munis stays in the garden for three months, restoring it and feeding the tree, Mahdokht. But in Neshat's film she never goes into the garden. She stops at its gates, deposits her delicate friend who has been physically and psychologically defiled, and immediately returns to Tehran to join the resistance.

Although uncharacteristic of Neshat's work to this point the didacticism within the film's deployment of history was intentionally directed at US audiences.[10] Although known in academic and political circles, CIA documents confirming US involvement were not declassified until August 2013, 50 years later and four years after the debut of *Women Without Men*. Just as Munis is moored to the radio, Neshat's own experience of the Iranian Revolution was from the spectatorial apparatus of media, in news and photos. *Women Without Men* reverses her role, creating history for viewers, realizing it as spectacle in her cinematic representation of the catastrophic fall of Mosaddegh. In the years after 9/11, she experienced marginalization as a Muslim American under an atmosphere of fear and Islamophobic while also watching a radicalization of Islam globally, the weight of politics permeating her life.[11] Through the politicization of Munis an American audience witnesses this part of Iranian history, and Iranians reflect upon the persistence of women against patriarchal repression throughout its history. However, Neshat's range of references are "an agent of the cosmopolitan and globalizing process of cultural osmosis" evidenced in her disclosure of "talking to Iranians about Iran, but also talking to Americans about America."[12]

In *The Politics of Spectacle*, Okwui Enwezor's essay for the Gwangju Biennale (2008), he addressed the post 9/11 media spectacularization of global anxieties and its fashioning of cultural power, asserting that the misguided responses and calculations of the US would result in the ebbing of its influence. Although he still espoused the potential of international exhibitions as spaces for political and critical reflection, he observed that artists were reorienting themselves from these centers and mainstreams toward transversal communities of practice in the "decline of the American brand." This should include its epistemological narratives and universality, against which new interpretive modes of history are required in concert with ethical approaches and the inclusion of its peripheral voices. In Neshat's film, American images, influences, and interventions abound and symbolize further its interruption into Iran's cultural and political life.

This is most evident in the story of Fakhri, the sophisticated wife of a Pahlavi general whose self-presentation and interests in society life are the most reflective of an Americanization of culture. Everything about Fakhri appears glamorous, from her Western-style dress and sunglasses to her cultivated circle of artists and intellectuals. By the time she hosts her first party at the orchard, it is public knowledge that American and British troops have aided the coup of Mosaddegh and the installation of the Shah. When Pahlavi's soldiers crash the party, they intimidate and inflect their power, taking over the dinner table and eating the food. But the commander asks Fakhri and her guests to sing Persian songs, and the guests and the soldiers relax together into the evening. While sitting with a young American woman, he waxes on the greatness of Iran in the Persian language she cannot understand, symbolically leaving that greatness untranslated. Unavailable to those still living under the Islamic Republic where the film is banned[13] the party scene is a reminder to diasporic Iranians of society before the Revolution while prefiguring the increasingly rigid autocracy that would follow.

While the other characters wear chador or floor-length veil in public, Fakhri chooses the more progressive rousari and manteau; at one point, a former lover comments how much she resembles American actress Ava Gardner. For the others, the veil leaves their bodies at key moments of their liberation: when Munis jumps from the roof and she finally takes to the streets with protesters; when Zarin slips into the orchard through a hole in its wall; and when Faezeh, empowered by her time in the garden, walks back to the city alone. As with much of her work, Neshat suggests women's bodies as liberatory sites, not as a Western model of freedom, but in its fluid possibilities for transgression itself, crossing and recrossing boundaries of even life and death to transcend its limitations. Therefore, Neshat treats Westernization of the period with ambivalent symbolism; images of Elvis Presley in Zarin's brothel and the sudden introduction of Fakhri's fluency in English invoke Western culture as omnipresent. Just as the upper-class Tehranis and the soldiers encroach on the private space of the orchard, the character bearing the greatest burden of patriarchy's socio-economic conditions, Zarin, falls ill and dies before the morning.

Zarin and the Problem of the Prostitute

Parsipur's themes of sexual, psychological, and corporeal oppression are perhaps most overtly fulfilled in Neshat's translation of Zarin (Figure 4.1). In the brothel scenes Zarin is clearly distraught; she stares distantly and lies motionless, disconnected from her physical existence. She ignores the cries from the brothel owner (a cameo by Parsipur) and won't leave her room. Finally, one of her clients appears faceless and she flees in terror to a public bathhouse. Ablution, or ritual washing, is an important Muslim custom necessary to cleanse the body before prayers inside the mosque and after certain activities, particularly sexual contact. The blue-gray palette of the scene, with mists of steam dispersing a mysterious film throughout the space, recalls the Orientalism of Ingres's *The Turkish Bath* (1862), but the recurrent image of mist, here and in Mahdokht's death/resurrection in the orchard's pond, compound the two in their shared desire to overcome their physical bodies. One without sex and one with too much, they each experience madness and disconnectedness to

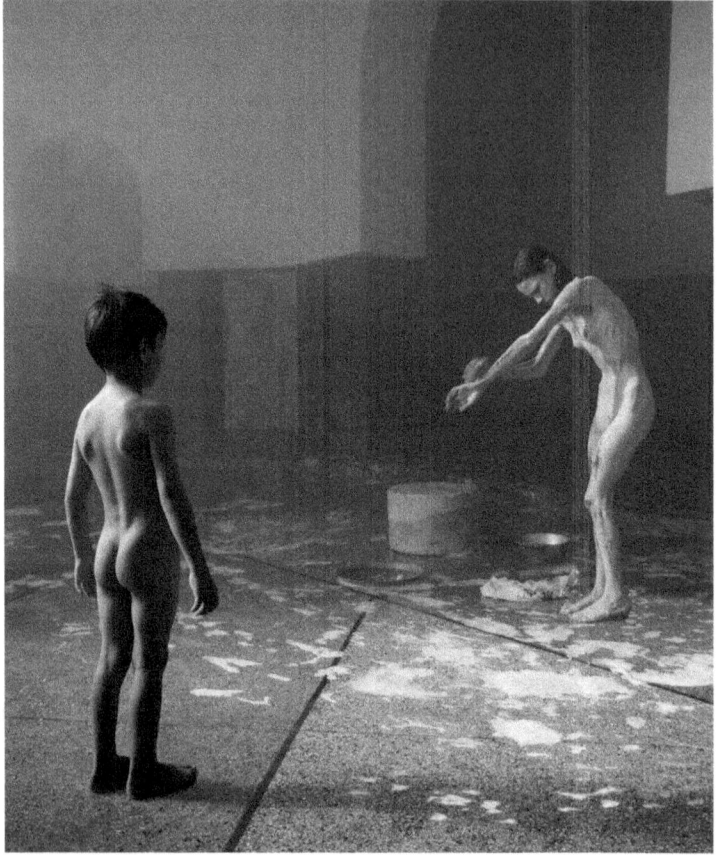

Figure 4.1 Zarin Series, 2005. C-print. 55×47 ½ inches (139.7×120.7). © Shirin Neshat. Courtesy of the artist and Gladstone Gallery.

their bodies that curator Beatrice Stammer described as "Zarin's overriding sense of her own impurity [that] leaves her as scarred as Mahdokht's purity leaves her."[14] An obsessive and unrealistic focus on virginity dehumanizes the female body and renders it as a contested, even political, site.

Zarin's body, or that of the Tehrani prostitute more generally, is the site of collective trauma at the intersections of religion, poverty, and complex societal attitudes regarding sex and the female body. In Iran, prostitution was regulated and taxed for centuries, but as with most societies its workers came from the poorest situations with little economic recourse. The official policy under both Pahlavi eras was to continue its regulation while driving it out of the public eye, to a space outside the city. Sara Reza has insisted that Zarin's street scenes "bear uncanny resemblance to Shahreno," the redlight district of the 1970s.[15] Still, prostitutes remained outcasts in a society that confoundingly co-prioritizes virginity and motherhood, and it was the worst possible fate for women. With the Constitutional Revolution (1905–11), the *Majlis* (consultative council) formed in 1906 and adopted a secular attitude toward socioeconomic reforms. As upper-class women became more outspoken in this period, the veil was criticized as a factor to blame for lower-class women's reliance on prostitution. A co-condition of veiling as a social practice barred contact with unrelated men in the public sphere, thereby excluding them from most economic opportunities. The confluence of poverty, poor education, and mandatory hijab were investigated for the first time as social conditions enabling prostitution and disabling the economic foundation necessary to a modern Iran.

Maryam Zehtabi Sabeti Moqaddam's insightful study of the prostitute in twentieth-century Iranian literature traces its socio-economic realities to its literary symbolism of religious dogmatism and patriarchal values. The prostitute became allegory for conditions that hindered the development of modern Iran in the waning of the Qajar dynasty. Called "social novels," they formed a shift in women's place in Iranian literature during the first Pahlavi era, and brought attention to arranged marriages, proscriptions surrounding virginity, and male prerogatives for polygamy and divorce, all of which were discoursed as contributions to prostitution and detractors to the development of the nation-state. In the second Pahlavi era, similar themes of prostitution brought to light the hypocritical disconnect between prostitution and marriage laws under Islam, which ostracized prostitutes while legalizing *mut'a* (temporary marriage). Prostitutes in the social novels of the early twentieth-century typically rendered sympathy and emphasized choices made due to economics, bound as they were to conditions of religion and patriarchy.

Under the Islamic Republic, Parsipur interrogated Shari'a law and its impact on women's lives by dispatching themes on prostitution, virginity, rape, and domestic violence. She also made deliberate word choices to affect the psychological and verbal violence used to subjugate and control women. Amir calls Munis a 'slut' after she has been outside the home, and insults regarding marriageable age such as 'old girl' or 'left-behind girl' are translatable to the English 'spinster.' Fakhri's husband cruelly attests that menopause puts her past the age of a desirable/desiring woman. Like Neshat, Parsipur enters a global feminist conversation by virtue of intercultural similarities, here in the importance of language to marginalize women. Before returning to the character Zarin, I focus here on verbal slurs to reign in the significance of 'prostitute' as meted out and weaponized by the Islamic regime toward women activists. Segueing dissidence from women by envisaging them as the socially outcast, morally shameful prostitute has been directed recently at women protesters who have removed their veils in the Woman.Life.Freedom movement. However, its use stretches to the Republic's foundation, notably with the May 1980 execution of Farrokhroo Parsa, Iran's Minister of Education who, among other charges, stood trial for "spreading prostitution." Under the IRI, prostitution is illegal; but thus appropriated, the 'prostitute' is not so much an economic issue, but a politicization based on traditionally misogynistic stigma used to silence women.

Zarin therefore bears specific socio-political and allegorical weight, further exemplified by her extreme corporeality that viscerally confronts the viewer with the isolation and shame of her sexual exploitation. To the shock of the women and children in the bathhouse, she violently scrubs her emaciated body until her skin bleeds, reclaiming it as an abject site of trauma and suffering. Although not described as such in the novel, her anorexic body in the film perhaps highlights conservative Islam's severe restrictions of women's bodies that compel them to self-regulate and self-scrutinize. Zarin's silence throughout the film bears resemblance to one of Neshat's early conceptual tools, symbolic of suppressing the voices of women who must bear the texts and signs inscribed upon her. A criticism of the film was that character development was subordinate to imagery, which certainly could be said of silent Zarin, allegory for the ways politics and religion co-conspire in the physical and psychological violence of women.

Corporeal Limits and Liminal Spaces

Particularly with Neshat's video installations, knowledge of self occurs through intersubjective exchanges, a transgressive practice contiguously framed by Foucault's crossing and recrossing at the limits. The embodied experience in liminal spaces – the cultural situations of exhibition or cinema – imbricate the consciousness of viewers attained, in the words of Maurice Merleu-Ponty, as 'flesh.' It is this relegation of embodied consciousness translatable to corporeality that Mulvey situates within 'transgressive cinema' which further manifests "the awakening of female characters to a world of sensation that profoundly alters and expands [their] access to and understanding of the web of social, economic, and cultural relations that shapes their environment."[16] The material nature of the film imbues this 'world of sensation' via stylistics of framing, depth of field, camera movement, color, and audio intensity to enhance the character's awareness of their relationship to the world – and the viewer's relationship to her through a careful emphasis of flesh. Neshat differentiates Tehran's cool, neutral palette with the warm, vibrant color of the orchard scenes, the bland uniforms of the army and the socialist protesters contrast with the women's floral dresses. Super 35 Color film maintained similar fidelity to Neshat's earlier practice with millimeter film, but its digital application of high-resolution and full-frame capabilities enhanced textures and color density and the cinematographic flexibility of subject framing. Slow dolly-zooms and aerial pans place the orchard in a temporal other-worldness, and the close-cropping of subjects' faces is reserved to the female characters.

An affective style of transgressive cinema, such as it arguably rests with Marks's affect theories of color, texture, and memory-artifacts that suggest tactility and stimulate the sensorial, can also assess Neshat's filmic visual language as aesthetic-political. For Beugnet, transgressive cinema forges a path between the haptic visual and feminist film theory, "detached from its object yet bent on interpreting, investigating, and visually 'consuming' the object of the gaze."[17] Neshat's earlier practice had sought to destabilize viewers between two visual fields, disrupting their spectatorial possession of the Muslim female. In *Women Without Men,* the chador is reduced as a visual sign, seen quite rarely as the characters are most often shot within the *andaruni,* of the home or brothel, and the practice was not compulsory in the period portrayed. Here, Neshat turns more attentively toward elements of tactility, emphasizing the materiality of the film before deep character analyses or precise plot development. The sensorial engagement with these allegorized subjects, used to express conditions of class and patriarchy, further embed Neshat's aesthetic-political approach within transgressive cinema.

The interplay of allegory and style visualizes Parsipur's magic-realist novel for the screen, and the film itself has been described as magic-realist, including by its filmmakers. Maria Walsh linked the immersive and affective, through attended gestures of color, sound, and movement, to the hallucinatory images of Surrealism.[18] Primarily a literary genre, magic-realism, as opposed to the art historical Surrealism, nonetheless binds the film's fantasy elements and visual intensity that suspends the spectator, embodied and liminal, grasping for meaning through the corporeal resonances played out on screen. Neshat's most obvious visual allusion to Surrealism are the faceless men, recalling Max Ernst or René Magritte (in the Parsipur novel they are headless). Rosa Holman's assessment of magic-realism's role in Neshat's adaptation is the creation of a third-space of 'nothingness,' evident in Munis's floating in-betweeness – heaven/earth, life/death – and made relevant by Frederic Jameson's idea of magic-realism not as a literary or visual style that supplements the real but an alternative reality itself, existing as magical and fantastical.[19] Thereby, the real and fantastic, the historic and the liminal spaces, collude in a narrative evoking transformation.

The orchard is healing and redemptive, but these conditions are also fraught by the necessary confrontations with memories of sexual violence. As Faezeh walks into the darkness of the orchard, she encounters an apparitional reenactment of her rape. One man holds her to the earth and the camera pans to her anguished face, leaving the violent actions of the second man off-screen. Unlike the original act, the confrontation is within her control; as a disembodied memory, it must be faced to be overcome. Later inside the home, she gazes at her nude breasts in a mirror, a character arc based in corporeal expressions that analogously transition from Kristeva's abject-repulsive to Foucault's erotic-transgressive body. Zarin, who "chose" a life of sexual exploitation has deeper wounds and, belonging to the lowest class, is more susceptible to shifts in her environment. Faezeh is excited for Fakhri's party, shedding her conservative hesitancies and symbolically embracing a new society under the Shah monarchy; but Zarin's illness, projected through an ever-weakened, emaciated, and feverish form, is an instinctive comprehension that this new society will not overcome class-bound distinctions of patriarchy. As an upper-class woman, Fakhri has welcomed and taken care of Zarin; but she goes on with her party knowing its degenerative effects, foreshadowed by a tree that falls from the garden, smashing through the living room window. The upper-class divorceé, Fakhri's disconnect with the low-class prostitute, Zarin, recalls the class differences between women that inculcated a divide between the Iranian-elite and Islamic-revolutionaries. Her corporeal presence is relegated to its adornment of high-fashion, a surface style indicative of the film's allusions to Westernization as ambivalent and contradictory sign, its cultural encroachment symbolized by Zarin's frail body and eventual death.

Throughout Neshat's work, woman's connection to nature may be an essentialist allegory, but it nonetheless anchors to longstanding Iranian and Islamic meaning that contradictorily celebrates and constrains women. For instance, in a simultaneously poetic yet ageist-sexist simile, Amir asserts that "A woman's body is like a flower. Once it blossoms it begins to whither." Holman divides the liminality of the women's shared space into three zones: the domestic garden where the women bond and regenerate; the orchard, providing a mysterious and haunted engagement with memory; and the desert beyond, the intermediary space with the outside world. The woman-as-tree, the lushness of the garden symbolic of fertility and female beauty, are less tangential allegories as they become locational counter-sites to the transformation of the characters. As the fantastical and the real collide between imagination and memory, their internal psychologies are expurgated in the processes of transformation. Somehow, Amir makes his way to the orchard on the night of the party to ask Faezeh to become his second wife. More empowered and aware of the misogyny of married life to a devout Muslim man, she rebuffs his offer. In the novel, Zarin merges with the gardener – metaphoric of men who respect and care for women, the kind man whose face she can see – and they rise as smoke into the sky. In Neshat's version, Zarin simply dies and Fakhri, grief-stricken, is left with the mess of the party to clean. Embittered by Zarin's death, Faezeh returns to Tehran the next morning, sauntering down the dirt path in her Western dress.

It is a rather bleak ending in contrast to the transformation of Parsipur's characters in the novel and is no different for the fate of Munis. Active side-by-side with her male colleagues of the oppositional movement she has, quite literally, come to life. The reenactment of these protests, filmed in Casablanca, feature people carrying images of Mosaddegh and signs translated as "down with the British." In the novel, such specificities are unaddressed, and Munis is more intellectually curious than politicized. Her transformation in the film occurs through her suicide, longing to be nationalist. In the novel, it is after reading a secular book on sexuality that she returns home and announces to their servant "I'm not the same person that I was before."[20] Quoting from the text, in the film it is Faezeh who informs her that virginity is a "hole not a curtain," a revelation to them both, whose understanding of their own bodies was hitherto disconnected by religious, patriarchal language and its obsessive restriction upon the female body, imbricating it with hijab itself. It's a moment in the film that goes otherwise unnoticed, as Neshat renders Munis's enlightenment as political rather than sexual, a device to explicate the film's historical events. After witnessing the death of a young Pahlavi soldier, stabbed by her closest comrade in the Tudeh Party, she becomes as disenchanted as Faezeh with her liminal space, her dreams for an Iranian nationhood die with that violent act. As she holds the soldier of the enemy in her arms, her final words of comfort to him are "Death isn't so hard. You only think it is." In circuitous fashion defying temporal logic, the film ends as it began with Munis's suicide. The emphasis on death may seem dismal, but intense transformations are necessary to transcend circumstances and invent new societies. Her final words narrate her slow descent and recall her time as a revolutionary, "We only wanted to find a new form... to find a new way."

Neshat's decision to use the character of Munis as a political and historical device imbricates fictional/fantastical spaces with historical/representational qualities, "pulling the referential image farther away from the real in order to return to the world a greater truth that would inhere in the image alone."[21] With regards to film as a format of spectacle, Erika Balsom might challenge Enwezor's refashioning of politics within the liminal spaces of exhibition,

> precisely because our news media have been converted to entertainment and our artistic media increasingly resemble entertainment, it is necessary to reassert the spaces of the gallery and museum as institutional and discursive sites that can contest the derealization of spectacle.[22]

Women Without Men was shown within the museum complex as well as distributed in theaters, as is the case with much intercultural and independent film. Rather than derealizing spectacle, it is the film's affectative qualities that most resonate its overarching use of history in service to revealing the ways in which the authority of religion and government affect women regardless of social class. This perhaps would not be as pronounced without Neshat's aesthetic-political commitment that instrumentalized the female body as corporeal material and communicated the spaces of regeneration as sensorially embodied.

The orchard may also be described as the liminal space of the diasporic subject, neither here nor there, where the pain and nostalgia of exile are not forgotten or forsaken to the possibilities of transformation or a transnational state of consciousness but persist alongside them. Corporeal disintegration from sexual exploitation and repression signifies domestic abuse, rape, and prostitution as forms of violence that are cross-cultural. Despite their specific causes from here to there, undergirded by religion, economics, and patriarchy they are collapsed in the psycho-social geographies of the film, hyper-realized by the Super 35 Color, anachronistic to the residue of black-and-white news-reels in the US that painted Mohammad Reza Pahlavi as a modernizing benevolent monarch or the grainy Super-8 captures of the Revolution. Recall-ing Marsha Meskimmon's "threshold sensory states," these psycho-social geographies remove the spectator from their media-spectacle knowledge of history and invert, through corporeal visuality, normative standards of gender repression through an intersubjective, embodied dialog with difference that allies itself to transnational feminist theory.[23] Bridging the chasm between fantasy and reality, *Women Without Men* invited viewers to transgress the lim-its of geography and realize the insistence of the past upon the present.

In September of 2009, Neshat was awarded the prestigious Silver Lion for *Women Without Men* at the Venice Film Festival and received wide critical praise at additional festivals before a limited distribution as an independent film in 2010. It presented a history new to American audiences while remind-ing diasporic Iranians of democracy lost. Its street protest scenes, with crowds standing against military guard and bearing images of their deposed leader, was an uncanny relevance to events that unfolded just two months before its premier. Clerical approval of a second term for Mahmoud Ahmadinejad was a devastating blow to civil liberties, let alone any dreams for an Iranian Repub-lic, sought since the Constitutional Revolution and briefly graspable under Mohammad Mosaddegh (1952–53). Strengthened by their fantastical circum-stances, Neshat's four women resist the injustice of their circumstances and oppose corruption, mirroring Iran's historical and contemporaneous reality.

Shahnama (Book of Kings)

The release of *Women Without Men* in August 2009 could not have been more prescient. On June 12, the Iranian Presidential election results shattered the hopes of a return to Reformist government after several years of rule under the conservative Ahmadinejad. It spawned the Green Movement, whose name derived from the green sash that former president Mohammad Khatami, the first Reformist president who lost to Ahmadinejad in 2005, passed to candi-date Hossein Mousavi. When Mousavi, popular especially among young vot-ers, lost to Ahmadinejad in a "landslide" victory up to three million people in Tehran alone immediately protested the suspected election fraud. The Green Movement swept throughout the country, demanding their civil liberties. Pre-dating and perhaps influencing the later Arab Spring that began in December 2010, it was the first large-scale protest movement that used social media. These new platforms made possible an immediacy of unfolding history, such as the shooting of Neda Agha-Soltan by the Revolutionary Guard, whose death-on-camera was filmed from a bystander's cell phone and transmitted globally. News on the uprising and the participation of women was produced with much more diverse, less politically filtered discourse than in the past.

Hamid Dabashi argues that the Green Movement returned Iran to a cosmopolitan political culture, underscoring its worldly connectedness to historic civil rights struggles.[24] The movement persisted despite the government's brutal playbook of expelling journalists, blaming foreign interference, torturing, raping, imprisoning, and murdering its citizens, until the final demonstration, on 14 February 2011, was violently suppressed. Although not intended as a political film, the timing of *Women Without Men* rendered it impossible not to unite its revolutionary narrative with current events, and the film was dedicated in its credits to all Iranians fighting oppression. In 2010, Neshat set out to create her first intentionally politicized body of work in an ambitious return to the photography that had begun her career. Now her subjects, men and women, were embellished with text from Hakim Abol-Qasem Ferdausi Tusi's *Shahnama* (ca. 977–1010ce), or *Book of Kings*, the epic poem of Persia's pre-Islamic rulers.

By referencing the *Shahnama,* Neshat aligns the globally recognized Green Movement with a classic of world literature, its activists with Iran's epic heroes. In some 50,000 rhyming couplets, Ferdausi recorded tales of 50 mythic and historical kings that had circulated orally for centuries, its earliest known visual representations painted on palace walls dating to the fifth-century.[25] It begins with Keyumars, the first king among humans, signifying the incredible longevity of Ancient Persia, from Cyrus to the Sasanians. At the crossroads of Eurasia, invaded by Arabs from the West in the seventh-century and Mongols from the East in the thirteenth, the *Shahnama* persisted and adapted to changes in linguistic and visual formats for centuries. Ferdausi's illustrated narrative cycles, widely disseminated, "became the key literary and visual targets of patronage by rulers who also needed to become 'Persian' in order to rule."[26] Written in Arabic script, its images were frequently produced by artists of the Mongol courts, and its tales not only produced identity and belonging but served as an instructional text, with examples of righteousness and good leadership to which rulers aligned themselves through commissions of its illumination.

Neshat's previous inscription of calligraphy onto the flesh of subjects in her photographs attest to the deployment of language and its psychological impact upon bodies that must bear or resist it. Further, Neshat's writing encoded the image as a performative practice, from staging poses to the careful application of calligraphy. In these new photos, one may imagine Neshat performatively standing in for the artisans of the *kitabkhana* (book house) who produced the text for royal patrons and with specific agendas of propaganda. Sussan Babaie also posits a complex relationship to the *Shahnama's* performativity, tied to its history of recitation in the public sphere and extended here to a contemporary spectatorship in the gallery space.[27] The series was divided into three parts: 45 portraits comprise the "masses," installed in an impressive grid;

several larger portraits of the "patriots," or those who participated directly in the protests; and three life-size "villains" whose scale indicates their dominance. The cultural importance of the *Shahnama* to Persian identity cannot be understated, the lines of its verse and the stories of its kings and heroes well-memorized by Iranians at home and of the diaspora. But one need not read the text to glean Neshat's comparison of its heroes to Green Movement activists or the failure of the current regime within Iran's much longer political history.

Each photo was taken by Neshat's long-time collaborator, Larry Barns, and printed as LE silver gelatin prints. The inscription of text, applied in acrylic, appears delicately in small fine lines across the exposed skin (faces and necks) of the bust-length portraits of the Masses, all wearing black shirts against a black background. A repetition of the stark, black-on-black format is repeated in the Patriots, but texts alternate between large, bold lettering on the faces and denser script overall. In three-quarters length portraits they each hold their right hand across their hearts as a universal gesture of patriotism.[28] Here, the text most closely visualizes early manuscript traditions of the twelfth- and thirteenth-centuries, with columns of text interrupted by blank vertical spaces. Texts on the Masses speak to a range of emotions when faced with tyranny, and the close adherence of the Patriot's to the *Shahnama*'s early textual visuality fuses its ancient meaning to their physical form. But all the subjects are unified in Neshat's signature direct gaze, and the overlay of text seems to imbue the portrait with profound silence/defiance.

The three Villains, an older man seated and two standing, represent the political and religious figures. Their shirtless torsos are decorated with the illustrated battle scenes from Mongol-style *Shahnama* texts. The black acrylic is punctured by splashes of red. Notably, in *Sheirif* (Figure 4.2) a foreshortened soldier's body falls diagonally, the neck cavity of his freshly decapitated head spilling forth blood. These figural scenes of battle appear similar to tattoo, which has continued from Ancient Persia into the modern era despite its prohibition under Shari'a law. The images upon Neshat's Villains bear resemblance to the practice among the Pahlavan urban athletes of the South, whose tattoos often reference the illustrated poems of Persian heroes from the twelfth- and thirteenth-centuries. Under Reza Shah Pahlavi, these wrestler-entertainers in the *Zurkhana* (gymnasium), provided a performative allusion to the heroic images they wore on their skin, a pre-Islamic or pre-Arabic image of the nation-state he desired to spread. However, images of the *Shahnama* hero Rustam intersperse with that of first Shi'ite Imam Ali, the Zurkhana patron saint.[29] This ambiguity of heroic reference is perhaps mirrored in the visual rhetoric of Neshat's Villains, inextricably identified with the atrocities of violence and military domination inscribed on their flesh and yet defying the Islamic government's restrictions upon tattoos and the Pahlavans' bare-chested exhibitionism.

This symbolic haziness imposes some consideration of Neshat's source images. The Pahlavan tattoos were most often based on widely available

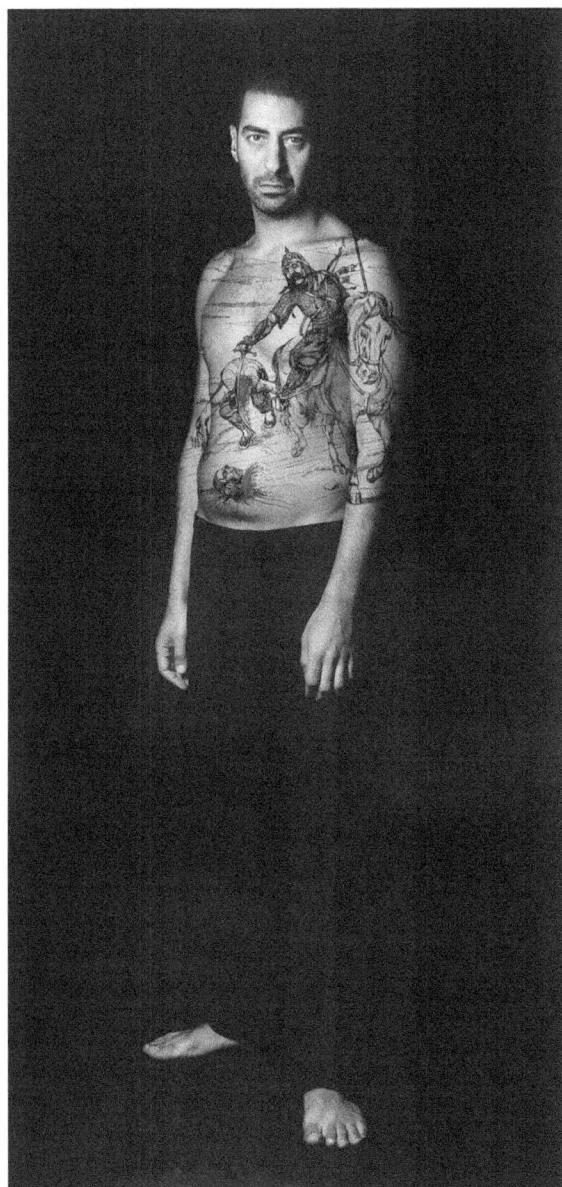

Figure 4.2 Sheirif, from the Book of Kings Series, 2012. Gouache on Paper, 99×49 inches (251.5×125.7 cm). © Shirin Neshat. Courtesy of the artist, Gladstone Gallery, and Noirmontartproductions, Paris.

lithographs, and exhibition catalogues have cited Neshat's appropriation from her own collection of early twentieth-century lithographic *Shahnama* texts. The earliest lithographic copies of the *Shahnama* were published in Bombay printing houses in 1846, then appeared in Tehran as early as 1848.[30] From late-medieval manuscripts to nineteenth-century lithographs, from hand-painted illuminations to copied drawings, from Mongol to Safavid and Qajar visual treatments, the *Shahnama* is foundational to Persian literary and visual culture and produces a public understanding of the world. According to Babaie, this "metavisual interplay across history" is uniquely Persian because the *Shahnama* has been profoundly integrated into Iranian daily life; its stories intermix, for instance, with modern propaganda murals on public walls communicating multiple ideologies and creating a culture of narrative visuality weaved into a collective consciousness.[31]

With her own signature admixture of text and figuration, Neshat reflects the complicated and multi-layered ideologies of the *Shahnama*. It bears reminding that early *Shahnama* manuscripts were commissioned by the courts, necessary to effectively identify themselves with Persian culture vis-à-vis their commission of rich illuminations celebrating the *Shahnama* tradition. At different periods of its history, certain images and stories were given greater attention and more frequent reproduction according to the context and required messaging. Therefore, productions of the *Shahnama* are also inherently politicized, and no less could be stated for Neshat's *Book of Kings,* intricately bound to its own context and communication with the spectator. This situates the *Shahnama's* ongoing contemporaneity within Iranian visual art practice, to which Hamid Keshmershikan has traced an evolution from the synthesis between a pictorial heritage of the past and modernism to the more recent, thinly veiled political and social commentary of contemporary artists.[32] Uniquely, the *Shahnama* straddles both these conditions, as contemporary artists turned to its culturally specific style, nationalist identifications, and political resonance in the years following the Green Movement and coinciding the text's 1000-year anniversary.

Neshat's treatment of the *Shahnama* is not a reimagination of its ancient tales but appropriated as a conceptual framework to imbue the Green Movement with historical import. The actual poems on the images are once again provided by modern poets who were suppressed and censored, who she thereby attributes with the same cultural and indentificatory significance as Ferdausi. They include Forough Farrokhzad, Mehdi Akhavan-Sales (1928–90), and Ahmad Shamlou (1925–2000), whose subversive works appropriately testament the tragic lives of creative resistance. Like Farrokhzad, Akhvan-Sales was persecuted under Mohammad Reza Shah. A supporter of Mosaddegh, he was imprisoned for a year in the 1950s, only to be persecuted again under the IRI. In similar fashion, Shamlou was also imprisoned in the early years of the Second Pahlavi era, only to be censored by the IRI as a "Westernized" poet, despite his role as an important translator of classical

Persian poetry. Neshat's anachronistic interruption of Iran's tradition with her transnational form, still speaking as she was to a global spectatorship from her exilic perspective, exhibits the same ambiguity as throughout her work, raising questions rather than answering them, revealing complexities and relinquishing oversimplifications. Although she asserts the importance of the *Shahnama* and replicates its visual layout, she excludes its verse for that of persecuted modern writers, their texts symbolically sealed to the flesh of Iran's new heroes, indicting the failures of all authoritarian regimes whose tyranny can never silence a nation's resistant voices.

Notes

1 Azari, Shoja and Shirin Nehsat. "In Movement: A Conversation with Shirin Neshat" in *Shirin Neshat, 2002–2005*. New York: Charta & Barbara Gladstone Gallery, 2005. p. 32.

2 Green, Tyler. "Trapped Between Two Worlds." *Los Angeles Times* (Oct. 9, 2005).

3 Transcribed from viewing. Gladstone Gallery, New York (July 8, 2009). Also included in the collection *Remembering the Flight: Twenty Poems by Forugh Farrokhzad*, trans. Karimi-Hakkak, Ahmad. Port Coquitlin, BC: Nik Publishers, 1997.

4 Heartney, Eleanor. "Heartney, Eleanor, Helaine Posner, Nancy Princenthal, and Sue Scott eds. Shirin Neshat: Living Between Cultures." *After the Revolution Women Who Transformed Contemporary Art*. New York: Prestel, 2007. p. 249.

5 Ebrahimian, Babak. "Passage to Iran: Shirin Neshat Interviewed." *PAJ: A Journal of Performance & Art*, vol. 24, no. 3 (Sept. 2002). p. 53.

6 Zanganeh, Lila Azam ed. "Interview with Shirin Neshat." *My Sister, Guard Your Veil; My Brother, Guard Your Eyes: Uncensored Iranian Voices*. Boston: Beacon Press, 2006. p. 49.

7 Beugnet, Martine and Laura Mulvey. "Film, Corporeality, Transgressive Cinema: A Feminist Perspective." p. 118. Mulvey, Laura and Anna Backman Rogers, eds. *Feminisms: Diversity, Difference, and Multiplicity in Contemporary Film Cultures*. Amsterdam: Amsterdam University Press, 2015.

8 Heartney, Eleanor. "Shirin Neshat: Interview by Eleanor Heartney." *Art in America* (June/July 2009). p. 157.

9 Shirin Neshat and Shoja Azari Interview with Sarah Mousley. Minneapolis: Walker Arts Center, 16 April 2010.

10 Ibid.

11 Hanson, Matt A. "An Iranian Artist in Exile Turns Her Camera to the West." *In These Times* (July 13, 2022). Web.

12 Bresheeth, Haim. "Shirin Neshat's *Women Without Men*." *Third Text*, vol. 24, no. 6 (2010), 754–758. p 757.

13 Shirin Neshat and Shoja Azari Interview with Sarah Mousley. Neshat revealed that bootleg copies were already available behind-counter in Iran.

14 Schmitz, Britta and Beatrice E. Stammer. *Shirin Neshat*. Berlin: Nationalgalerie im Hambruger Bahnhof & Museum für Gegenwart. 2005. p. 124.

15 Reza, Sara. "Travelling Light." *n.paradoxa*, vol. 17 (2006), 30–35. p. 35.

16 Beugnet, Mulvey. "Film, Corporeality, Transgressive Cinema: A Feminist Perspective." p. 193.

17 Ibid, 194.

18 Walsh, Maria. "'You've got me under your spell:' The Entranced Spectator." Trodd, Tamara ed. *Screen/Space: The Projected Image in Contemporary Art*. Manchester: Manchester University Press, 2011. p. 114.

19 Holman, Rosa. "Holding a Mirror to Iran: Liminality and Ambivalence in Shirin Neshat's *Women Without Men.*" *Screening the Past*, no. 38 (2013), p. 6.
20 Parsipur, Shahrnush. *Women Without Men.* p. 74. New York: The Feminist Press at the City University of New York, 1998. (Talattof and Sharlet trans.)
21 Balsom, Erika. *Exhibiting Cinema in Contemporary Art.* Amsterdam: Amsterdam University Press, 2013. p. 170.
22 Ibid., p. 182.
23 Meskimmon, Marsha. *Contemporary Art and the Cosmopolitan Imagination.* New York: Routledge Press, 2011. p. 7.
24 Dabashi, Hamid. *Iran, the Green Movement, and the USA: The Fox and the Paradox.* New York: Zed Books, 2010. p. 142.
25 Babaie, Sussan. "Visual Recitations: Neshat's 'Persian' Arts." Babaie, Rebecca R. Hart, Nancy Princenthal eds., *Shirin Neshat.* Detroit, MI: Detroit Institute of Arts, 2013. p. 30.
26 Ibid.
27 Ibid., p. 35.
28 Artist Statement. Ho, Meliessa. *Shirin Neshat: Facing History.* Washington, DC: Smithsonian Books, 2015. p. 163.
29 Shafiei, Shadi. "Tattoo Culture of the Zurkhana." Wrightson, Erica ed. *In the Field of Empty Days.* Los Angeles: Los Angeles County Museum of Art, 2018. p. 60–62. Much of this insightful information is indebted to Shafiei's concise entry.
30 Roxburgh, Donald J. and Mary McWilliams. *Technologies of the Image: Art in 19th-Century Iran.* Cambridge: Harvard Art Museums, 2017. p. 59
31 Babaie, Sussan. "Visual Recitations: Neshat's 'Persian' Arts."
32 Keshmershikan, Hamid. "Reflecting the Past into the Present versus Constructive Specificity in Modern and Contemporary Art in Iran." Komaroff, Linda. ed. *In the Field of Empty Days.* Los Angeles: Los Angeles County Museum of Art, 2018. p. 49.

Conclusion

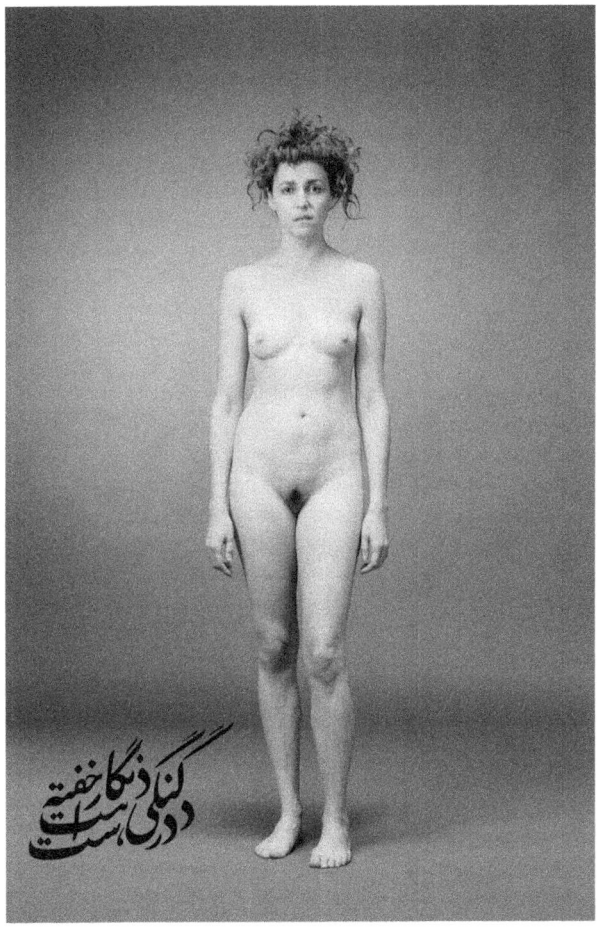

Figure C.1 Mariya, from *The Fury* Series, 2023. Digital c-print and acrylic, 75×50 inches (190.5×127 cm). © Shirin Neshat. Courtesy of the artist and Gladstone Gallery,

DOI: 10.4324/9781003341192-6

Nostalgia had sutured Neshat's pain of absence from Iran. But moving around the world to create and exhibit work affirmed her nomadic strength, no longer in longing for return.[1] Openly supportive of the Green Movement, a moment to which she felt compelled to respond, Neshat finally embraced being a political artist – but not only toward conditions in Iran. After *Book of Kings* premiered in January 2012, she left Iran as a subject and focused her critical attention toward the Arab Spring and the immigrant experience in the US, turning her gaze upon her adopted country for the first time. For more than a decade she has investigated other cultures and other problems.

Once again, however, history has intervened. At the writing of this volume, protests were culminating into a new revolutionary movement in Iran. On 16 September 2022, Mahsa Jina Amini was arrested and beaten by the *Gasht-e Ershad* (Guidance Patrol, or colloquially 'morality police') for failing to wear hijab to appropriate standards. She later died of her injuries, sparking a wave of protests throughout the country, rallying the cry *Zan, Zendegi, Azadi* (Woman.Life.Freedom) in further protests across the globe. The cosmopolitanism Hamid Dabashi had characterized for the Green Movement has redoubled, the world mesmerized by veilless women in the streets and awestruck by those protesting despite penalties as brutal as death. Neshat's film *Women Without Men* and *Book of Kings* photo series conferred her as a global advocate for the rights of the Iranian people. Now, Neshat allowed her earliest body of work – the 1993 *Unveiling* series (pictured in Figure 1.1) – to be rearticulated as public art.

The next month, a banner unfurled from the roof of Neue Nationalgalerie in Berlin, picturing Neshat's defiant forward-gaze and a split in her chador revealing text on her neck and chest in an improper display of the body. The intervention utilized the titular piece of that early exhibition, *Unveiling*; writ large on its banner "Woman.Life.Freedom" in English attested the movement's international scope. In November, a second photograph from the series, *Offered Eyes*, was painted onto the open-air staircase of Four Freedoms State Park on Roosevelt Island in the East River. Part of an installation of 16 works by Iranian artists demanding the removal of the IRI from the United Nations' Commission on the Status of Women, a demand successfully realized in the December U.N. vote. Strategically located across the waters from the U.N., the image was suited to the initiative's theme, *Eyes On Iran*.

Neshat began her newest series, *The Fury*, in April 2022, months before the Woman.Life.Freedom movement. Returning to an Iranian subject matter of which she had grown weary,[2] she nonetheless felt compelled to address Iran's protests of 2019–20. Incited by high fuel costs and inflation partially attributed to European and US sanctions, at least 1500 people were killed in a series of protests that began in "Bloody November." Opening at New York's Gladstone Gallery in January 2023, the image *Mariya* (Figure C.1) is one of five life-size nudes, four women and a young girl, standing against a gray backdrop. The bodies are of diverse proportions, and the inclusion of the young girl notes her particular and historic vulnerability to the sexual violence of patriarchal religion. Noticeably absent is the veil, no longer the basis for the visuality Neshat was calling into question. Rather, Neshat's first female nudes, juxtaposed again to the words of Forough Farrokhzad, locate the body as a contradictory site of abuse and desire, *Mariya's* text states that she is so consumed by her own dreams that she is lost from sight, essentially disappearing from the world in a deliriousness of love for another person. A second set of five large-scale photos depict close-ups of faces and nude forms with a minute application of Persian text that weaves in and out of legibility, adding textural effects consistent with chiaroscuro. The resulting gray tonalities are appropriate to the converse conditions of the body as vulnerable/confident, desiring/desired, and loved/abused.

Personally outraged by reports of the persistent rape of detainees during the Bloody November uprisings, Neshat created a new two-channel, black-and-white video, *The Fury* (Figure C.2). Political imprisonment has been a subject of her work, but *The Fury* directed attention to the sexual abuse of political prisoners rather than censorship of creative dissent. This return focus on Iranian women is also a return to the embodied practice of her first trilogy. A woman dances seductively, presumably for the man in portrait-view on the opposite screen. In one poignantly relevant take, she puts on a long black wig before she begins her provocative dance; its close resemblance to chador seems obvious, but later as she runs through the city streets wearing only underclothes, her hair is short, and the public cutting of hair is a recent act of protest by women in Iran. The narrative swings back and forth temporally, in the insistence of dream or memory, and it becomes clear that she is traumatized by sexual violence perpetrated by the same man she had seemed to seduce. Representing a militant authority or the Iranian government itself, he has betrayed her in an ambiguous moment when, in the warehouse where she has been made to dance for an entire room of similarly officious men, he blows cigarette smoke into her face. By means of some flawless editing, she staggers back from him covered in bruises.

Metaphors continue to structure a narrative progressed by a lyrical female voice filling the room and relinquishing character dialog. Imbricating the viewer and recalling another early signature of Neshat's motifs, a point-of-view shot captures the woman's spinning in circles before escaping the warehouse and onto the city streets of the opposite screen, clearly filmed in Brooklyn. Rather than locate a substitute site for Iran, the setting is Neshat's home of Bushwick, a neighborhood with a diverse demographic that the traumatized woman encounters and who observes her with suspicion and disregard. Finally realizing what has happened, a riot ensues in outrage, but loud drumming proxies their screams. As Neshat yet again witnesses history in Iran unfold from abroad, she has also expressed anger over the recent rise in White Supremacy and ill-treatment of immigrants in her adopted homeland of the US. *Fury's* new filmic location recalls American protests after the death of George Floyd

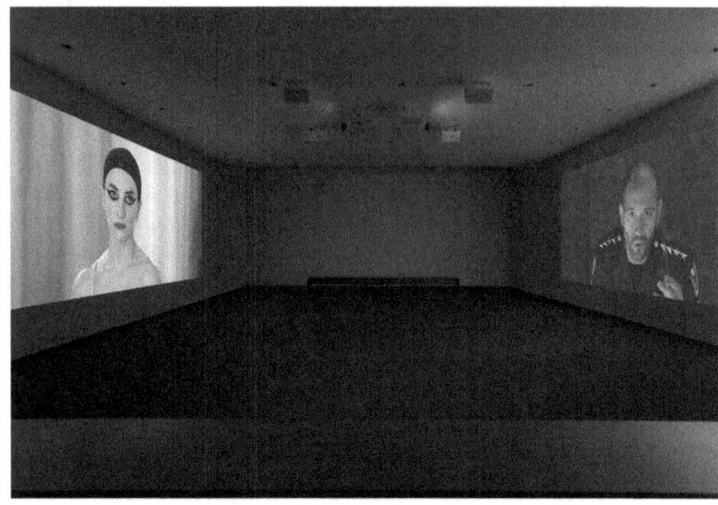

Figure C.2 The Fury, 2022. Two-channel video/sound installation. HD Video Mono-
chrome. Duration: 16 minutes and 15 seconds. Installation View of *Shirin
Neshat: The Fury*, Gladstone Gallery, New York, January 26–March 4,
2023. © Shirin Neshat. Courtesy of the artist and Gladstone Gallery.

that, like Woman.Life.Freedom, was a protest of many brought from outrage
for the one. Embedding fury for the woman's exploitation and rape within
Neshat's Brooklyn community, she positions these two civil rights movements from her dual, transnational conscience.

When I first encountered her work, I asked myself "If I enjoy these images,
am I the colonizer?" Yinka Shonibare, who has positioned his own aesthetic
practice as that of a "trickster at home with confusion" has stated, "Beauty
is political when it is appropriated by the 'Other.'"[3] Neshat has crafted a
specific aesthetic-political practice of "beauty and mystery" bound to "the
inter-relationship of human beings and their environment"[4] that compels us
to transgress the limits – the unspeakable, the untranslatable – of memory and
history, toward an experience that words and images often fail. Do theories of
embodiment, intersubjectivity, responsible/response-able viewership actually
work in practice – toward an empathic viewership? For me, because I can only
speak to my own embodied experience, Neshat's works required the commitment of an intersubjective *working* beyond the initial encounter that has lasted
decades and is perhaps some evidence that they do. What has always drawn
me to transnational artists, those who are from one geography but, for reasons
enforced or freely chosen, live and produce work in another, is their *unique*
and often objective perspective. They generate new meaning from the refuse

of a world at the whim of governments, restore power at the margins, and even reveal ourselves to ourselves.

Notes

1 Hanson, Matt A. "An Iranian Artist in Exile Turns Her Camera to the West." *In These Times* (July 13, 2022).
2 Jansen, Charlotte. "Why Neshat Is Turning Her Gaze Away from Iran." *Elephant* (Feb. 25, 2020).
3 Jones, Caroline A. *The Global Work of Art.* Chicago: Chicago University Press, 2016. p. 229.
4 Neshat, Shirin. MFA Thesis Exhibition Statement (August 1982). University of Berkeley Art Museum & Pacific Film Archive.

Index

Note: *Italic* page numbers refer to figures.